THE
LITTLE
BOOK
OF
WALES

MARK LAWSON-JONES

First published 2013

The History Press
The Mill, Brimscombe Port
Stroud, Gloucestershire, GL5 2QG
www.thehistorypress.co.uk

British Library Cataloguing in Publication Data.
A catalogue record for this book is available from the British Library.

ISBN 978 0 7524 8927 8

Typesetting and origination by The History Press
Printed in Great Britain

8

My trips around Wales continue to give me a sense of *belonging*. I tried to explain this feeling of Welsh pride, and it wasn't that easy. Luckily, the Welsh have a rather good word for it.

Hwyl (hu:il) is described in the Welsh University Dictionary *Y Geriadur Prifusgol Cymru* as: 'A healthy physical or mental condition, good form, one's right senses, temper, mood, frame of mind, nature, disposition.' It goes on to say that the word means 'a journey, progress or revolution.' A task completed with 'gusto, zest and fun.'

That was it! I had discovered something quite special.

diverse and wonderful landscape, the long and exhilarating history, the musicians, poets, writers and great thinkers of their age. I would need to write about Welsh links with the world and 100 other things. It would be quite a task!

A few years ago I started to visit museums, exhibitions and historic sites in Wales with two friends who have a love of history. It wasn't too long before I was mesmerised by my own nation and culture, its history, treasures and language. I would regularly return home in the evening with a jumble of facts, figures and stories, trying to put them all in order and make sense of all this new information. It was as if I had been a *stranger in my own land*.

There was a reason for this. When I was a schoolboy in the Welsh Valleys, history lessons would consist of learning about the kings and queens of England, the Romans, Normans and Vikings, Shakespeare, Queen Victoria and a bit of the First World War if we were lucky. We never really learned about the great amount of history on our own doorstep.

A quarter of a century later I would learn that the window which I used to stare out of in history lessons overlooked the route of the Chartists, when they marched past on 4 November 1839, calling for votes for ordinary working people. I hadn't been taught about them in school, and far from being an insignificant event in the life of my small nation, it was hugely significant. This last rising against authority to take place in Britain came to a gruesome end in Newport when they met the army.

I also didn't realise that the landscape, with its scars of industry, the sites of long-gone iron works, pit heads and spoil heaps, had fuelled the Industrial Revolution throughout the world, and the now green hills were very different 200 years before.

INTRODUCTION

How hard can it be? It's a book about Wales! I said to myself as I put pen to paper to start writing *The Little Book of Wales*. After all, I'm Welsh, I live in Wales, and I love all things Welsh...

It wasn't until I started to write this book that I realised how difficult it would be. My greatest fear would be that my *Little Book* would be nothing of the sort. Other books on Wales run to encyclopaedic lengths not to omit, misrepresent or offend. I would need to remember all the things I love about Wales and put them into some sort of order. So I sat and thought ... and thought some more ... and then some more. I would need to write about the

ACKNOWLEDGEMENTS

Thanks are due to several people: David Osmond and Richard Frame, who have explained to me how great Wales is; Clare Barratt who has given me a love of the Welsh language; my dad, Peter, who helped greatly with this book; and last but not least, my family, who put up with me and my 'great' ideas.

CONTENTS

CROESO I GYMRU – WELCOME TO WALES

So, what's so special about Wales then?

Thanks for asking. There is no escaping the fact that Wales is an extraordinary place.

With around 3 million residents, this country with an area of just over 8,000 square miles might seem a rather small place. However, in the league tables of the nations Wales punches well above its weight in many ways. It can't be denied that Wales and the Welsh have had an extraordinary effect on the world.

This astonishing land bordered by England, the Irish Sea and the Atlantic Ocean has produced artists and writers, academics, religious figures, adventurers and rogues to tell the story of Wales and the Welsh. The pages of history are full of their tales.

So, who are these famous Welsh people?

There are lots of them! They include: Richard Burton; Sir Anthony Hopkins; Sir Tom Jones; Catherine Zeta-Jones; Dame Shirley Bassey; Timothy Dalton; Charlotte Church; Roald Dahl; Tommy Cooper; and King Henry VII. Here are some others you might not have heard of:

Robert Recorde (1512-1558), the mathematician and physicist, born in Tenby, Pembrokeshire, invented the 'equals to' sign and the 'plus' sign, which first appeared in the book *The Whetstone of Witte,* published in 1557. This wasn't an end to the talents of Recorde though; in an extraordinary career, he was also appointed Physician to King Edward VI and Queen Mary, and Controller of the Royal Mint before being sued for defamation by a political enemy and dying in the King's Bench Prison, Southwark in June of 1558.

A Welshman even invented tennis! At a meeting of the Cambrian Archaeological Association, London, in August 1887, a Colonel Mainwaring made the following statement: 'I should like it to be entered on record that the now popular game of lawn tennis was the old Welsh game of *Cerrig y Drudion.*' The colonel's remarks came at a time when lawn tennis was enjoying a tremendous amount of popularity both in Britain and in the United States.

If that wasn't enough, Welshman Sir Pryce Pryce-Jones (1834-1920) from Newtown, Montgomeryshire, created the first mail order business in the world. Pryce-Jones hit upon a unique method of selling his wares. People would choose what they wanted from leaflets he sent out and the goods would then be dispatched by post and train. It was to change the nature of retailing throughout the world. Florence Nightingale, as well as Queen Victoria and royal households across Europe, bought from Pryce Pryce-Jones. At the height of his success he was selling to America and even Australia, and by 1880 he had more than 100,000 customers.

Mount Everest was named after Welsh surveyor and geographer Colonel Sir George Everest (1790-1866) from Gwernvale, Breconshire. Sir George was largely responsible for completing the Great Trigonometric Survey of British India, which ran from South India to Nepal. The Royal Geographical Society named Mount Everest after him in 1865, ignoring his objections that the name Everest could not be written in Hindi, nor pronounced by natives of India.

All very clever people! Is there anything the Welsh can't do?

It's worth mentioning the success Welsh people have had on the high seas too.

In 1170, it is said, Prince Madoc, with thirteen ships and 300 men, sailed from Llandrillo-yn-Rhos to America. The great explorer Columbus annotated his notes from the gulf of Sargasso with 'these are Welsh waters' on his return from America in 1492. There is believed to be linguistic and archaeological evidence to support an early Welsh colonisation of America… but more about him later!

A few centuries later a Welsh sailor diversified to a different type of seafaring…

Bartholomew 'Black Bart' Roberts (1682-1722) was probably the most successful pirate of all time; in the three years between 1719 and 1722, he captured and looted over 400 vessels, terrorising merchant shipping from Newfoundland to Brazil and the Caribbean and the African coast. No other pirate of his age comes close to that number of captured vessels. He was successful in part because he thought big, usually commanding a fleet of anywhere from two to four pirate ships which could surround and catch victims… and who thought all pirates needed a West Country accent? Arr, me hearty!

So much for the famous Welsh people! I thought Wales was only famous for difficult-to-pronounce place names?

Well, that's true too. The wonderfully named, *Llanfair-pwllgwyngyllgogerychwyrndrobwllllantysiliogogogoch* is a town in North Wales, which translates as 'the church of St Mary in the hollow of white hazel trees near the rapid whirlpool by St Tysilio's of the red cave'. It is believed to be the longest place name in the world.

Has Wales got any short place names?

Well yes, it's a tie between the many places in Wales with three-letter names:

Cog, in the Vale of Glamorgan, is one of the places in Wales with the shortest name, and the close-by Ely in Cardiff. Further north Hem in Montgomeryshire, and the beautiful town of Usk in Gwent are all uncommonly short for Welsh place names. The most common short name in Wales is Cwm: the name appears everywhere. In Welsh, *Cwm* means valley, and there are lots of those.

Speaking of Welsh, you haven't mentioned the language yet!

According to the 2011 census 19 per cent of residents (526,000) speak Welsh fluently. English is spoken in all areas, and the law requires both languages to be given equal treatment. The Welsh language is very old, probably spanning the last 1,500 years. This could make it the oldest language in Europe.

Tell me some astonishing facts!

Ok, how about this: in Wales, on 13 May 1897, Guglielmo Marconi (1874-1937) sent the first ever wireless communication over open sea. It traversed the water from Lavernock Point to Flat Holm Island, a distance of 3.7 miles (6km). The message read, 'Are you ready?'

Wales is the only nation in the United Kingdom not to be represented on the Union Jack, and sheep outnumber humans 4 to 1.

There are more castles per square mile than any country in Western Europe.

Finally, the poet Brian Harris sums up the Welsh spirit, or *Hwyl*, in the first verse of his 1967 poem *In Passing*:

To be born in Wales,
Not with a silver spoon in your mouth,
But, with music in your blood
And with poetry in your soul,
Is a privilege indeed.

'WELSHNESS' AND THE WELSH

'Welshness' is a sort of indefinable quality that is something like a mixture of national pride and a sense of place. It is the

feeling that, however diverse we all become in Wales, we have something special that joins us. It may stem from the great sense of belonging and community the Welsh have. I've no idea how we can measure *Welshness*, but some people have tried, to no avail.

The 2011 census returned some interesting results for the people of Wales:

Two-thirds of people who live in Wales consider themselves to be Welsh, with the Valleys area of *Rhondda Cynon Taf* having the most people who say they are Welsh. In a nutshell, 75 per cent of residents were born in Wales, 20 per cent in England and 5 per cent somewhere else.

The most recent census also showed that there had been a small decline in the number of Welsh speakers in Wales. Now 19 per cent of the population speak the language, compared to 21 per cent in 2001. Although the traditional areas of Carmarthenshire, Ceredigion and Gwynedd all report only a small reduction, the most anglicised areas, like Monmouth and the rest of south-east Wales, report a small increase in Welsh speakers.

A century ago, it was a different picture. Most people spoke Welsh, and English was not only rarely heard, a large amount of people couldn't speak English at all.

Since 2001, the population of Wales has been slowly rising; there has been a 5 per cent increase to 3,100,000 people.

2

THE LAND AND
THE LANGUAGE

SO WHAT DOES WALES LOOK LIKE?

Wales looks very good; it is bordered by England to the east
and the Atlantic Ocean and Irish Sea to the west. It has an
area of 8,022 square miles (20,779 sq. km). The capital and
largest city of Wales is Cardiff, with a population of 350,000.

Wales has at least fifty-three islands not far from the coast. The largest of these is Anglesey (*Ynys Môn*) in the Irish Sea, which has an area of 260 square miles; the smallest is the tiny Cardigan Island at 0.06 square miles.

Wales is mountainous with the highest peak, Snowdon (*Yr Wyddfa*), standing at 3,560ft (1,065m). There are three mountainous regions: Snowdonia, situated in the north-west; the Cambrian Mountains in mid-Wales; and the Brecon Beacons in the south. The mountains assumed their present shape during the last Ice Age, the Devensian glaciation.

CLIMATE

Wales has a temperate climate. This basically means that it never really gets very hot and never gets really cold. Winters are mild and summers are warm, and it seems to rain more than anywhere else! In north-west Wales, around 2m of rain falls each year. The sunniest month is May, averaging 188 hours of sunshine, and the warmest months are July and August.

Most travel guides tend to make a comment that reads something like: 'waterproofing advised throughout the year.'

THE COASTLINE AND
THE WALES COASTAL PATH

On 5 May 2012, the 870-mile (1,377km) coastal path around the whole of the Welsh coast was officially opened. The Wales Coast Path (*Llwybr Arfordir Cymru*) twists continuously from Chepstow in the south to near Queensferry in the north, following the dramatic scenery, cliffs, sandy bays and ancient castles.

This prompted the *Lonely Planet* guide to declare: 'What a wonderful thing: to walk the entire length of a country's coastline, to trace its every nook, cranny, cliff-face indent and estuary.'

They also put *Coastal Wales* at the top of their list of World Regions to visit.

The coastal path visits two national parks, eleven nature reserves and dozens of Sites of Special Scientific Interest (SSSIs).

Starting in North Wales, the coastal path follows the Dee Estuary along the coast to the Isle of Anglesey. The beautiful scenery here gives way to the rugged views of Snowdonia. Ceredigion and the expansive Cardigan Bay, buffeted by the winds and the sea, is a great place to watch nature. Pembrokeshire's beaches and the seaside towns of Tenby and Saundersfoot have been a centre for the great Welsh holiday for generations. Continuing around the coast, we arrive in Carmarthenshire with its proud and long history. The Gower peninsular was named as Britain's first Area of Outstanding Natural Beauty in 1956, and from here the industrial heart of Wales starts with Swansea, Port Talbot, Cardiff and Newport. The coastal path ends in the border town of Chepstow.

OFFA'S DYKE (CLAWDD OFFA) AND THE OFFA'S DYKE PATH

If the coastal path wasn't spectacular enough, Offa's Dyke is a great frontier earthwork built by Offa, King of Mercia, from AD 757 to AD 796. It was built to form some type of boundary between the kingdom of Mercia and the Welsh kingdom of Powys. In places it is still up to 65ft wide and 8ft high. It runs almost the whole length of Wales.

Each year hundreds of walkers travel the length of the Offa's Dyke path taking an average twelve days to complete the 177 miles (285km). They stay in pubs and bed and breakfast accommodation, or camp along the route. Traditionally, walkers start at the marker stone on the Dyke at Sedbury Cliff, 1 mile from Chepstow on the banks of the Severn Estuary, and complete the journey at the marker stone on the Prestatyn seafront, on the banks of the Irish Sea.

They witness the beauty of mountains, hill pasture, river valleys and lowland fields. Over 30 per cent of the journey is within three Areas of Outstanding Natural Beauty and 9 per cent is within a national park. Two thirds of the trail is in Wales. It passes through no less than eight different counties and crosses the border between England and Wales twenty-seven times.

Although the Dyke was constructed over 1,200 years ago, the path was only officially opened on 10 July 1971, by Lord Hunt, leader of the 1953 Mount Everest expedition.

THE LANGUAGE AND THE PEOPLE

Many languages are spoken in Wales: English is the most common and Welsh (*Cymraeg*) is second, with almost a fifth of the population speaking the language. After decades of decline in the early twentieth century the Welsh language is slowly returning in many areas. The widespread provision of Welsh-medium education and a flourishing media and arts industry has certainly assisted this. S4C, the Welsh language television channel, and BBC Cymru, producing drama, news coverage, documentaries and current affairs and sports in Welsh, have recently renewed a strategic partnership to produce programmes for several more years.

Bilingual policies, adult education and legal rights for the language have all assisted with the expansion of Welsh in Wales.

Don't worry though; you certainly don't need to speak any Welsh to enjoy a holiday or a business trip to Wales. But just a little understanding of the language will bring your trip to Wales to life.

If you want to have a go at Welsh pronunciation, however, this next section might be for you.

Welsh is a great language to learn, because, with virtually no exceptions, it is pronounced as it is written. There are no tricky and fiddly heteronyms like in English – just think of *buffet*, *colonel*, *abuse*, *rebel*, *use*, all having different pronunciations and meanings, but the same spellings. In Welsh, if you see it – you say it!

HERE ARE SOME OF THE DIFFERENCES BETWEEN THE ENGLISH AND WELSH LANGUAGE

b, d, h, l, m, n, p, ph and **t** are all pronounced as in English.
c – pronounced as a k, as in English 'cane', but never as in 'city'
ch – pronounced as in the Scottish 'loch', but never as in 'chain'
dd – pronounced th, as in the English 'the'
g – pronounced as a hard g, as in the English 'grip'
ll – is pronounced a bit like th
f – is always pronounced as a v, as in the English 'van'
ff – is pronounced as an f, as in 'off'
r – don't forget you need to *roll your r's* in Welsh
rh – is aspirated in welsh as in 'perhaps'
w – pronounced like oo, as in 'spoon'
y – has a couple of sounds, but don't worry they are easy to learn. The first is 'ur', when you use it as the *definite article*. *y castell* (ur casteth) is 'the castle'. Secondly, *Gwynt* (gwint)

means 'wind' and gives us a regular 'i' sound. The phrase *y Cymro* (er cum-ro), meaning 'the Welsh', has another sound, an 'um'.

Welsh has no k, q, v, x or z.

Ok! We are nearly there. Just a few more rules:

I at the beginning of a syllable, like English y as in yes. Iorwerth *(yore-worth)*

A – short as in English cat (not as in cape), or long as in English bar. Dda *(thar)*

E – short as in English hen, or long as in English panel

I – short as in English pit (never as in like)

O – short as in English not (never as in book), or long as in English robe *(Goch)*

U – short, rather like the English I sound in pit (never as in hut), or long like a French u or as in English meet

Y – represents two distinct vowel sounds, 'obscure' and 'clear'

Right! Got it? Here we go…

WELSH LANGUAGE IDIOMS AND PROVERBS

These little gems tell us a lot about the Welsh philosophy and culture. The knowledge and experience of the old, wise words in austere times, and the importance of *chwarae teg* (fair play), are all found here.

Idiom	Direct Translation (Meaning)
Nerth gwlad, ei gwybodaeth	The strength of a nation is its knowledge

Henaint ni ddaw ei hunan	Old age comes not on its own
I'r pant rhed y dwr	The water always runs into the valley *(The rich tend to get richer)*
Gŵr heb bwyll, *llong heb angor*	A man without a sound mind, a ship without an anchor
A'i waed yn berwi	His blood boils *(He is angry)*
A ddarleno ystyried	Let him who reads reflect
Mae e'n Gwybod *Hyd ei Gyrn*	He knows the length of his horns *(He knows his weaknesses)*
Gwna dda dros ddrwg, *uffern ni'th ddwg.*	Do good over evil and hell will not steal you
A ddialo air hagr, *rhoed ated têg*	To revenge a harsh word, give a gentle reply
Mae fe'n lladd gwair	He is cutting hay *(He is killing time)*
Pan fo llawer yn llywio *fe sudda'r llong*	When many steer the ship will sink
A ddwg angeu nid adfur	What death takes it will not restore
Canu cyn borefwyd, *crio cyn swper*	Sing before breakfast, weep before supper

Mae hi wedi llyncu pry	She has swallowed a fly *(She is pregnant)*
Mwyaf y brys, mwyaf y rhwystr	More the hurry, more the difficulties
N'ad fi'n angof	Forget me not
Llaeth I blentyn, cig I ŵr, cwrw i'r hen	Milk for a child, meat for a man, beer for the old
Hedyn pob drwg yw diogi	The root of all evil is laziness
A ddywedo pawb, gwir yw	What everyone says is true
Tri chysur henaint: tân, te a thybaco	Three comforts of old age: fire, tea and tobacco
Tri chynnig I Gymro	Three attempts for a Welshman
Mae hi'n siarad trwy hi het	She's speaking through her hat *(Talking rubbish)*
A elwir yn gall a gais fod yn gall	He who is called wise will seek to be wise
Siared pymtheg y dwsin	Speaking fifteen to the dozen *(To speak very quickly)*

And one of my favourites...

Mae hi'n bwrw hen wragedd a ffyn	It's raining old ladies and sticks *(Heavy rain)*

THE WELSH 'NOT' –
AN UNHAPPY HISTORY

In the nineteenth and early twentieth century in Wales, it was believed that Welsh was an unsuitable language to teach children, so in many schools it was actively discouraged.

If a child was heard speaking Welsh, they were required to wear a wooden plaque with the letters 'WN' ('Welsh Not') inscribed. If another child spoke Welsh, the plaque would pass to them. At the end of the day, or in some cases the end of the week, the child left wearing the plaque would be severely punished. It was believed that this would ensure children would only speak English in school.

The origins of the belief that Welsh was an unsuitable language probably dates back to the *Blue Books* published in 1847. This parliamentary report on the role of Welsh language included the paragraph: 'The Welsh language is a vast drawback to Wales, and a manifold barrier to moral progress ... it is not easy to over-estimate its evil effects ... there is no Welsh literature worthy of the name.'

For correctness, it's worth mentioning that the *Blue Books* state that the 'Welsh Not' was both arbitrary and cruel. Nevertheless, the practice flourished, and this symbol continues to be associated with cultural oppression by many in Wales.

3

WHEN DID WALES HAPPEN?

In his book the historian John Davies suggests that around AD 500 the people of Wales were organised into an 'heroic' society celebrated by the chroniclers and poets. When the Romans finally left Britain something of the Empire survived, and the people maintained the political structures they had inherited.

Around AD 425-450 Vortigern ruled over much of the former Roman province that stretched across the Midlands and Wales, and he enjoyed great success. He adopted a rather cunning plan to keep his kingdom safe: he allowed invaders to settle, as long as they promised to sort out his other enemies. So, the British tribes the Votadini and Gododdin people fought to stop the Irish invading, alongside Vortigern and his people. Even the feisty Saxons were allowed to settle, as long as they helped to stop the Picts invading.

The partnerships were very powerful, and stories of bravery and courage were passed down the generations. One of the oldest known pieces of British literature is a poem called *Y Gododdin*, written in Old Welsh, previously passed down via the oral traditions of the *Brythonic*-speaking Britons. This poem celebrates the bravery of the soldiers from what was later referred to by the Britons as *Yr Hen Ogledd,* the Old North.

The early kingdoms of Wales have older roots than the kingdoms in England. Gwent was founded first, and grew from a Roman settlement in the south. A local tribe, the Silures, reasserted their power and created a society in the south-east corner of Wales.

The rulers of Gwynedd in the north traced their ancestors to Cunedda Wledig, his name meaning *the holder of lands who is like a hunting dog*. He was believed to be the leader of the Gododdin people, when they settled in AD 450.

Powys may have been formed from the lands of the Cornovii people. In south-west Wales, Dyfed, the land of the Demetae, came under the rule of Irish settlers, as did the kingdom of Brycheiniog.

All this battling, building and bargaining was taking place all over Wales, as the foundations of the nation were being set.

Although the English ruled most of lowland Britain, they continued to advance north and west between AD 650-750. They caused a great deal of damage, especially in the kingdom of Powys. However, as they looked up at the Welsh mountains and considered the immense task of trying to take the lands there by force, they realised that they had run out of steam.

King Offa of Mercia understood that a line must be drawn. No one is quite sure why, but an extraordinary monument which runs for 177 miles (285km) was constructed from sea to sea. This huge earthwork, called Offa's Dyke, might have been constructed as a defence against the wild and restless Welsh, or it might have been to show where the boundary was. Whichever it was, it is by far the most stunning construction of the age.

WELCOME TO WALES –
CROESO I GYMRU

This new physical boundary brought a sense of unity, shared purpose and self-awareness for the Welsh. This new age saw almost all of the people west of Offa's Dyke led by the same ruler, Rhodri, king of Gwynedd, who by his death in AD 877 had added Powys and Seisyllwg (Cardigan and Carmarthen) to his kingdom. Rhodri was given the title *Mawr*, meaning 'The Great', because of his victory over the Vikings in AD 856. Apart from a few notable examples of places with Viking names like Swansea, Anglesey and Fishguard, and a little light pillaging and raiding of the monasteries near the coast, the Vikings had very little effect on Wales and the Welsh. This wasn't so with the English, whose whole system was destroyed by the continued invasions of the Vikings, and eventually rebuilt under the leadership of King Alfred and the House of Wessex. This was a violent and turbulent time in history: battles were commonplace and thousands were killed, with many more displaced from their homelands. The death of Rhodri Mawr came in a battle with the English in AD 878.

In Wales, after the death of Rhodri Mawr, the unity between the north and Seisyllwg was broken. A century of uncertainty passed until unity returned, brought by Rhodri's descendant Hywel, an extraordinary diplomat and political figure, who added Dyfed and Brycheiniog to the fast-expanding union. Hywel too was given a title like his grandfather.

Hywel Dda or 'Hywel the Good' codified the Welsh Law. It was not 'king-made-law' but traditional, concentrating on unity and reconciliation in disputes between individuals and families. The Law of Wales was written, according to tradition, at Hendy-gwyn (Whitland) probably around AD 940. For centuries, being bound by the Law of Hywel Dda was a sign of being Welsh. Hywel had a steady reign, and avoided bloodshed, unlike his grandfather, by attending the English Court and recognising the English king.

THE LAW AND HYWEL THE GOOD

Following Hywel Dda's death in AD 950, the new ruler Gruffudd ap Llywelyn brought about a highlight in Welsh history, when by AD 1057 he had united the whole of Wales under his authority. Dyfed, Seisyllwyg and Brycheiniog were joined together and called Deheubarth, and the nation was complete.

After years of relative peace, however, Gruffudd ap Llywelyn, not known for his diplomatic skills or peaceful nature, invaded lands the Welsh had lost centuries before far to the east of Offa's Dyke. In retaliation, Harold, Earl of Wessex, invaded Wales in 1063 and Gruffudd was hunted down and killed. Three years later William, Duke of Normandy, seized the throne of England.

After 1066, Wales was once again a violent and dangerous place: the internal struggles for power and the sense that Wales was crumbling led to much disunity. To make things worse, the English king, worried about the aggressive and leaderless Welsh, created earldoms in Shrewsbury and Hereford, appointing men with military knowledge and experience of war.

The dominant ruler in Wales at this time was Bleddyn ap Cynfyn, who was king of Gwynedd and Powys.

The Norman attacks on the Welsh were greatly damaging and brought about the downfall of the kingdom of Gwent before 1070, and by 1074 the forces of the east of Shrewsbury had captured Deheubarth and much of the land around Offa's Dyke.

In 1075, Bleddyn ap Cynfyn was killed; this gave way to civil war, allowing the Earl of Chester to take most of Gwynedd.

In the south, William the Conqueror advanced into Dyfed, founding castles. The Norman Conquest was virtually complete.

In AD 1094, however, there was a general Welsh revolt, and by 1100 the Normans had been driven out of Powys, Ceredigion and Gwynedd.

A strong kingdom was built in Gwynedd under Gruffudd ap Cynan. In AD 1136, there was a crushing victory in Crug Mawr and the Normans were routed. The internal political struggles and disunity in England meant that the Welsh were able to extend their borders further than ever.

Not much has been mentioned about Powys, mainly because their strong ruler, Madog ap Maredudd, kept the peace until his death in 1160. In the south the four sons of Gruffudd ap Rhys ruled Deheubarth in turn, and eventually won the kingdom back from the Normans. The youngest of the four, Rhys ap Gruffudd, also known as The Lord Rhys, ruled from ad 1155-1197. In 1171, Rhys met King Henry II and came to an agreement with him to pay a tribute, and was later named Justiciar of South Wales. Rhys is responsible for holding the first festival of poetry and song at his court in Cardigan over Christmas 1176, which is generally believed to be the first eisteddfod, an institution which remains an important part of Welsh culture to this day.

LLYWELYN THE GREAT

Back in the north, a power struggle had arisen, which produced one of the greatest Welsh leaders of all time. Llywelyn ap Iorwerth, also known as *Llywelyn Fawr* (the Great), was the sole ruler of Gwynedd by 1200, but it was in the next forty years that he effectively unified Wales.

Llywelyn made his capital at Abergwyngregyn on the north coast, overlooking the Menai Strait. When he died in 1240, King Henry III would not let his son Dafydd ap Llywelyn take over the agreements that were in place. War broke out in Wales in 1241 and again in 1245.

To avoid challenges, Dafydd had imprisoned his brother Gruffudd, who was the rightful heir to Llywelyn under Welsh Law. He was handed over to King Henry III, to be sent to the Tower of London. However, during a daring escape attempt one night in 1244 he fell 90ft to his death, after tying sheets and linen together. Sadly, the improvised rope broke and the Yeoman of the Guard found him at the foot of the White Tower in the morning. The window has been bricked up, but can still be seen in the Tower to this day.

His brother, Dafydd, died suddenly in 1246 leaving no heir.

PRINCE LLYWELYN

Gruffudd had four sons, Owain, Llywelyn, Dafydd and Rhodri, and after their uncle's death there was a battle between them. Llywelyn was eventually successful, and Llywelyn ap Gruffudd (or Llywelyn the Last Leader) came to power.

The Treaty of Montgomery, in which King Henry III of England recognised Llywelyn as historical Prince of Wales, was signed in 1267 and confirmed Llywelyn's control over a large part of Wales, and peace reigned for a period in Wales. Wales was a nation with a prince, living in harmony with neighbours and looking to the future. It was a good time in Welsh history.

In 1272, all this started to change. With the death of King Henry III in 1272, King Edward I came to the throne. Prince Llywelyn was considered to have been given too much power, and the new king sought to control the Welsh once again. War followed in 1277. Llywelyn had to negotiate again, and the Treaty of Aberconwy was signed. This new treaty was nothing like the Treaty of Montgomery; it greatly constrained Llywelyn's ability to rule all of Wales.

Difficulty in keeping his family and the lesser princes under control became a huge problem when his brother Dafydd ap Gruffydd attacked Hawarden Castle in March 1282. This rising spread to other parts of Wales and eventually Llywelyn was dragged into the conflict and fought with Dafydd. Tragedy had struck for Llywelyn at this time when his wife Eleanor de Montfort died giving birth to their daughter Gwenllian. With nothing to lose, Llywelyn then left Dafydd and took a force south, trying to rally support in South and mid-Wales.

In the mid-Wales town of Builth Wells, on 11 December 1282, Llywelyn was killed while separated from his army. Accounts differ as to what happened, but the general belief is that Llywelyn was tricked.

The first account states that Llywelyn approached English forces after crossing a bridge. Hearing the sound of battle, he quickly turned to rejoin his army, but was struck down by a lone lancer from the north of England, who didn't realise whom he had killed. It was some time until a knight recognised the body as that of Llywelyn. This information came to light some fifty years later in the north of England.

Monks who supported Gwenllian, Llywelyn's daughter, who was exiled after the death of her father, wrote the second account in the east of England. They described how Llywelyn, at the front of his army, was approached by the leaders of

n, in 1399, Richard II of England lost the throne to ry IV, the Lord of Monmouth, Brecon, Kidwelly and nore. Many of the powerful Welsh and northern English ilies had close links with King Richard, and they treated the king with suspicion. The legitimacy of the English Crown in question and there were rumblings and talk of revolt.

the opposing army, who promised that he would receive their homage. This was a trick, and his army was immediately set upon. He was separated from them with a small retinue of eighteen, which included clergy. At dusk they were ambushed and chased into a wood at Aberedw. Llewelyn was attacked and struck down. He called for a priest, giving away his identity. He was then killed and beheaded. His brother Dafydd continued battling but was arrested a year later and hanged, drawn and quartered at Shrewsbury.

Llywelyn was the last Prince of Wales before Edward I made Wales England's first colony. At Cilmeri, near Builth Wells, there is a monument and memorial to Llywelyn. A plaque reads 'Near this spot was killed our Prince Llywelyn 1282'. He is held to be one of the heroes of the Welsh people to this day.

THE AGE OF CASTLES AND THE ENGLISH 'PRINCE OF WALES'

Things had changed. King Edward I of England started to build a string of heavily fortified castles around Wales, which would keep the restless and violent Welsh quiet, and would also serve as symbols of his power and authority.

At this point in history, Wales was almost part of England, even though it had its own customs and language. However, to further underline this point, the Statute of Rhuddlan was signed by the king, effectively bringing an end to the Welsh Law in 1284. Seventeen years later, in 1301, there was a curious event in Welsh history.

Legend has it that the king had promised the Welsh people he would announce a 'new born prince of Wales', who would not speak a word of English, and would have been born on Welsh soil. The Welsh people were excited about

this prospect, and they looked back to the rule of Prince Llywelyn, when there was peace.

To their great vexation, King Edward made his own son and heir the Prince of Wales, investing him 'Edward Caernarfon'. This story might be fanciful, because it dates only to the sixteenth century, and speaks of a time when the English Royal Court, and indeed the English Aristocracy, spoke Norman French, and, of course, a newborn baby would speak neither English nor Welsh. Was this a royal joke?

As you might expect, there were a number of risings against the English throne during this period. Some Welsh leaders made pacts with the French to invade England and free Wales from the English rule.

THE RISING OF OWAIN GLYNDŴR

Around 1354, a Welsh nobleman, Owain Glyndŵr (Owain Glyndyfrdwy, Owain of the Valley of the Dee), was born.

David Hanmer, a powerful Marcher Lord, prob him, sending him to London around 1375 to stu Inns of Court. Upon returning to Wales, he marr Hanmer's daughter, and was made Squire of Glyndyfrdwy, with all the responsibilities that er

Glyndŵr was well respected in English societ only a squire, but also a lawyer who spoke fo In 1386, he began serving in the King': Richard II in France and Scotland. In his m he undertook garrison duties on the English-S near Berwick-upon-Tweed, then went to soutl and the Channel for a sea battle off the coast a Franco-Flemish-Spanish fleet was defeatec career then took him to the short sharp Bat Bridge in December 1387. Returning to his after the death of his father-in-law, Glyr military action in three very different theatr without a doubt, well versed in the art of wa he was the embodiment of the perfect highb part of English society and culture.

However, there were some things that ma about Glyndŵr. On his father's side, he dynasty of Powys. On his mother's side he w of Lord Rhys of Deheubarth, and by 1378, law in London, he became the last Welsh title Prince of Wales, following the line o was killed nearly 100 years before.

The poet Iolo Goch described the house in grew up as a 'mansion of generosity'. It the English border in Sycharth, although owned homes at Glyndyfrdwy in the Dee Wales. Glyndŵr was educated as an Engli also knew the customs, laws and practic the Welsh.

Th
He
Og
far
ne
wa

All fires start with a spark, and the same is true for wars, revolutions and risings. The new king had failed to intervene in a dispute between Glyndŵr and a neighbouring landowner and the dispute became quite heated. It then appears that on 16 September 1400 a small band of Glyndŵr's supporters proclaimed him Prince of Wales in the church of Saints Mael and Sulien, in the town of Corwen. Those present included his eldest son, his brothers-in-law and the Dean of St Asaph.

Shortly afterwards a group of Glyndŵr's supporters attacked English settlements in north-east Wales and then melted away into the mountains, and so the Glyndŵr rising began.

After a few skirmishes between King Henry IV and Glyndŵr's followers in September and October 1400, the war began to spread. Most of mid and North Wales supported Glyndŵr and King Henry appointed Henry Percy, the famous 'Hotspur', to bring order to the country. However, the fighting still raged and the English army was losing ground on many fronts.

In 1401 Good Friday fell on 1 April, and the Tudur brothers of Anglesey, cousins and supporters of Owain Glyndŵr, devised a cunning plan to make a real breakthrough by doing something so daring that it is remembered to this day as an act of genius.

Rhys and Gwilym ap Tudur ap Goronwy and a company of just forty men tricked their way into the walled town of Conwy. The castle was part of the string of huge fortifications built by King Edward I in the thirteenth century in an effort to subdue the Welsh. Some say they were disguised as workmen or simply mingled with the country folk who would enter the town to trade in the market.

The Good Friday three-hour-long solemn 'prayers at the cross' were taking place in the parish church of St Mary, and the garrison soldiers were in attendance. Upon hearing a commotion outside, the soldiers ran out and were quickly subdued by Glyndŵr's men and the Tudur brothers.

With forty men, they had demonstrated true stealth and cunning, showing how the pinnacle of military architecture could fall in an instant. The castle was now in the hands of Glyndŵr and the rising of the Welsh people.

Henry Percy (Henry Hotspur) was helpless and recognised that he would have to agree terms with the rebels, and within three months he had offered full pardons for all involved in the daring raid, apart from Glyndŵr and his close family.

The Tudurs turned their back on Glyndŵr and they gave up the castle, and eight of Glyndŵr's soldiers were executed as part of their deal with the English. This betrayal hit hard at the rising and Glyndŵr himself.

The rising went 'back to basics'. The savage and unpredictable attacks were becoming more accurate, and the drawing back into the vast mountains became a signature of the supporters of Glyndŵr. As time went on, the king led several campaigns against him, but his strategies made little headway against the guerrilla tactics of the Welsh and their prince. At one stage, the king believed that his enemy even had control over the weather, such was the precision of their attacks, which usually caught his army at a disadvantage.

In an act of frustration, the English Parliament passed the *Penal Code*, which prohibited the rebellious Welsh from gathering together, gaining access to office, carrying arms and dwelling in fortified towns, with the same restrictions being imposed upon Englishmen married to Welsh women.

Shortly after, King Henry recalled thousands of troops from Shrewsbury and Hereford into South Wales; they confiscated Welsh properties and executed many of Glyndŵr's men. At the same time, he ordered the sacking of the monastery at Strata Florida and the execution of the monks resident there. During the attack, Glyndŵr's men set upon Henry's army, and they returned to Hereford with nothing to show for their efforts.

In October 1401, Henry 'Hotspur' Percy, the Justiciar of North Wales, left for Scotland, and in his absence Glyndŵr was free to attack Welshpool and even capture the baggage train of King Henry. A month later, Glyndŵr attacked Caernarfon Castle, and flew the flag of Uther Pendragon, King Arthur's father, but in a bloody and violent battle he lost 300 men.

The king's Parliament needed to consider peace, but those with influence who had lost lands to Glyndŵr rejected any compromise and demanded action. Meanwhile, in Wales, the appearance of a brightly burning comet led the Welsh to believe that Glyndŵr had almost magical powers. They believed that he was the true heir of the great Welsh rulers of the past, and his support increased hugely.

In August 1402, King Henry invaded with, it is said, 100,000 men from Chester, Shropshire and Hereford in a three-pronged attack. Glyndŵr's men stayed out of the way and continued their stealth attacks. The weather turned once again, and the English army returned empty handed and in abject chaos.

Back in London, even though the English Parliament passed new laws, they were to no avail. The support for Glyndŵr amongst the Welsh continued to grow and the rising benefitted from the defection of hundreds of Welsh bowmen from the English army, who could no longer, in conscience, kill their countrymen.

At the lowest ebb in the rising for the English, an alliance was formed between Glyndwr and the Mortimer family (who believed they were usurped as rightful heirs to the English throne by Henry), when a member of the Mortimer family married Glyndŵr's daughter Catherine. An agreement was reached that if King Richard was still alive, and returned, then they would crown him King of England and Wales. If he were dead, then one of the Mortimers would take the crown. One historian wrote:

> By the end of 1402 the rebellion was really heating up, and the action became truly national. In 1403 Glyndwr headed to the south and the west. His forces marched down the Tywi Valley gaining support as they went. English castles and manor houses fell in their wake. Indeed Carmarthen Castle fell to the Welsh. He then headed West attacking Glamorgan and Gwent. Abergavenny and Usk Castles were attacked and burnt before taking Cardiff and Newport.

With Glyndŵr in South Wales, Prince Henry of England, the future king and hero of Agincourt, burned the family homes of Glyndŵr in the north at Sycharth and Glyndyfrwdwy in retaliation, and many local people were captured and executed.

In June 1403 all the English borderlands were fortified in the expectation of a Welsh invasion of England. The 8,000-strong army of Glyndŵr was given the keys to Carmarthen Castle. It can be argued that this turn of events was the total collapse of English rule in Wales. Then, out of the blue, Henry 'Hotspur' Percy returned from Scotland and with his father, the Earl of Northumberland, pledged his support for Glyndŵr and the Mortimers. He gathered support from the Cheshire-Welsh and rode to Shrewsbury to support the rising there. At the time, King Henry IV was heading north to Scotland and met his son Prince Henry at Shrewsbury. They arrived first and forced Henry 'Hotspur' to fight before his reinforcements arrived.

On 21 July, their combined forces defeated the army of 'Hotspur', who was killed in the battle. Over 300 knights and up to 20,000 men were killed or injured.

In April 1404, Harlech Castle fell to the Welsh, as did Aberystwyth Castle. Glyndŵr set up a court and described his vision for a Welsh Nation. He then called a Parliament in Machynlleth in the presence of envoys from France, Scotland and Castile. It was in this month that he was crowned Owain IV, Prince of Wales. After this milestone event in the history of Wales and the Welsh, Glyndŵr's own envoys agreed a treaty with the French, because the sympathetic French King Charles VI was the son-in law of the deposed King Richard II of England.

Within two months, sixty French ships and 700 men had sailed from Brittany and Normandy, raiding the coast of England with Welsh troops on board, setting fire to Dartmouth and pillaging the coast of Devon.

In February 1405, a *Tripartite Indenture* was signed in Bangor, North Wales, by Owain Glyndŵr, the Earl of Northumberland and Edmund Mortimer; they decided to divide all England into three parts:

> Glyndŵr would take Wales and the West of England, including Cheshire, Herefordshire and Shropshire. Edmund Mortimer would take all of southern and western England, and the Earl of Northumberland would take the north of England as far south as Warwick, Norfolk and Northampton.

One year later, the tide began to turn. Glyndŵr suffered defeats in the Monnow Valley and his eldest son Gruffudd was defeated and captured near Usk. He was taken to the Tower of London, where he died. Glyndŵr's brother Tudur was also killed at Usk, where it was reported that Prince Henry ordered the beheading of 300 Welsh prisoners in front of the castle after the battle.

In June 1405, the English sailed from Dublin and attacked Anglesey, forcing Glyndŵr to retreat to Snowdonia and the mountains. However, a month later the balance was redressed when 2,500 French landed at Milford Haven joining Glyndŵr's 10,000. Together they marched to confront King Henry in Worcester, where a standoff lasted for eight days, and in a mystery that remains to this day, Glyndŵr returned to Wales with his army.

Power was definitely in the hands of the Welsh, and the next year saw many more military and diplomatic victories for Owain Glyndŵr, Prince of Wales.

But in 1406, the Welsh started to lose battles, as the French withdrew their help. An independent Wales wasn't part of their plan, as their only goal was to invade and subdue England. This difficulty was compounded by the death of the Earl of Northumberland in Yorkshire. Then, in 1408, Harlech and Aberystwyth castles were besieged by the English.

In March 1409, six months after the onset of the siege of Harlech Castle, many were dying through starvation or illness, including Edmund Mortimer. Although Glyndŵr and his only surviving son Maredudd escaped, the rest of his family was captured, including his wife Margaret and his two daughters, and three Mortimer grandchildren. All were taken to the Tower of London and died there.

In 1410, Glyndŵr escaped capture again, whilst raiding on the Shropshire border, but some of the leading figures in the rising weren't so lucky and were either killed or imprisoned. Then, in 1412, Glyndŵr led one of his final and most daring raiding parties. With his most loyal soldiers he cut through the king's men, and captured a leading Welsh supporter of King Henry, Dafydd Gam (Crooked David), in an ambush in Brecon. This was the last time that Glyndŵr was seen alive by his enemies. As he had done nine long years before, he disappeared to the mountains, this time to live on in the imagination of the Welsh people and their culture. Glyndŵr left the question of what might have been.

WHAT HAPPENED NEXT?

Even though there were colossal rewards offered for information leading to the capture of Owain Glyndŵr he was never captured or betrayed, and he also ignored offers of royal pardons.

Tradition has it that he soon died and was buried possibly in the church of Saints Mael and Sulien in Corwen, where it all began, or in the estate of Sycharth. There is also a theory that he lived the rest of his life on the estate of his daughter Alys's husband in Kentchurch, south Herefordshire. Her husband, Sir John Scudamore, was the king's appointed Sheriff of Herefordshire, and had somehow avoided the rising and remained in office.

In his book *The Mystery of Jack of Kent and the Fate of Owain Glyndŵr*, Alex Gibbon writes that the folk hero *Jack of Kent*, also known as Siôn Cent, the family chaplain of the Scudamore family, was in fact Glyndŵr himself. Gibbon points out a number of similarities between them, including physical appearance, age, education and character. So, perhaps Glyndŵr passed himself off as a Franciscan friar and family tutor, living the rest of his life with his daughter. After all, he was described as a master of disguise during the rebellion, which he used to avoid capture and gain advantage over the enemy.

The Owain Glyndŵr Society (*Cymdeithas Owain Glyndŵr*), formed in Carmarthen in 1996 to prepare for the 600th anniversary celebrations, make three statements about this enigmatic Welsh prince:

– Owain was one of the greatest patriots Wales has ever known.
– His name has become a symbol of pride and freedom.
– He sacrificed everything for a dream of Wales as a nation,
governing itself with its own institutions and universities.
Where he died is not known, and the location of his grave
has become one of the great mysteries of Welsh history.

WALES AFTER OWAIN GLYNDŴR

For fifty years the balance of power in Wales changed very little. The Wars of the Roses started in 1455 between the two rival branches of the House of Plantagenet, Lancaster and York. Thirty years after the fighting began, the victory

went to Henry Tudor, whose claim was on the Lancastrian side. Henry had landed in Wales in 1485 and rode to Bosworth, defeating Richard III in battle. He was crowned King Henry VII, the House of Tudor subsequently held power in England and Wales for nearly 120 years.

Henry VII was born at Pembroke Castle in west Wales in 1457, two years after the Wars of the Roses started. Henry made some shrewd moves, exploiting his Welsh ancestry, and gaining military support on the way to the Battle of Bosworth. He had come from an old, established Anglesey family whose name had been written in Welsh history previously.

Henry VII was descended from Rhys ap Tewdwr, the King of Deheubarth in South Wales, and more recently he had relatives who sided Owain Glyndŵr in his revolt. Even though the links could have been stronger, the Welsh Bards declared that he was *y Mab Darogan* (the Son of Prophesy), and he was given their support.

I'M HENRY THE EIGHTH, I AM

It's difficult to imagine what the Bards must have felt when his son, King Henry VIII of England, came to the throne in 1509. Henry did not have the same love of Wales that his father had. Henry VII had a Welsh dragon and wolfhound on his heraldic insignia. Henry VIII dropped the wolfhound and replaced it with a lion, removing a link to Wales.

It wasn't long before Henry's attention turned to the Marcher Lords, and how they managed their lands. He was convinced that they didn't control the criminals and bandits who operated in the Welsh Marches (the border area between England and Wales); he felt that the Lords were taking bribes from criminals who would escape by returning to Wales to avoid English justice. Henry also became annoyed that the mostly Roman Catholic Lords frowned upon his divorce from Catherine of Aragon, and disagreed with his clash with the Pope. So, Henry decided to take action, starting with taking full control of Wales, removing all power from the previously powerful Marcher Lords.

Between 1536 and 1543, the English Parliament then passed a series of laws that together became known as the Acts of Union. Wales became one land, and the Marches disappeared from the political map. Wales was then divided into counties and each one had a Justice of the Peace, appointed from London. The Welsh legal system was annexed to England, and the administrative system of Wales, unchanged since 1282, was brought to an end. Some civil matters were heard in local courts, but the incorporation of Wales led to England becoming a modern sovereign state. So how did Wales look after 1542?

Five new counties were established: Monmouthshire, Brecknockshire, Radnorshire, Montgomeryshire and Denbighshire, thus creating thirteen Welsh counties, with a Justice of the Peace appointed to each county. The borders of Wales were established, and have not changed since. This was an unintentional side effect of the Acts, because it was thought that Wales would just become a part of England at the time. The Court of Great Sessions was established in Wales, and a High Sheriff was appointed to each county.

These changes were extremely unpopular with the Welsh gentry, although some privately believed that it might make Wales a more peaceful land. It seems that the price of this *peace* was an expectation that the Welsh people would forget their culture and identity, their past and their pride.

Modern historians believe that the average Welsh citizen would have suffered significantly, being expected to trade and survive in a system that was alien to him or her.

The Welsh language suffered also. The first section of the 1535 Act states: 'the people of the same dominion have to do daily use a speech nothing like ne consonant to the naturall mother tonge used within this Realme.'

Section 20 of the Act goes on to make English the only language of the law courts and states that those who spoke Welsh would not be appointed to public office.

Under the terms of the Acts of Union, Wales was represented in Parliament, but Welsh MPs were not truly representative of the people in their constituencies and Welsh was not spoken in Parliament.

Wealthy Welsh families made sure their sons only spoke English and sent them to London in an effort to advance their careers.

Henry was attempting to force all Welsh people to be *English* and tie them to London in terms of loyalty. If you wanted to make your way in London either politically or socially, as a young Welshman you had to drop any sign of Welshness.

It seems that the Welsh had no response to these measures. With such a hugely powerful and enigmatic king, leading a massive army in the nation next-door, they were largely silent. King Edward I's symbols of English dominance, the string of castles, were still standing.

The Welsh didn't and couldn't complain loudly.

WALES FROM 1553

In 1553, when Henry's daughter Mary became the Queen of England, she tried to undo many of the changes her father had made, especially in relation to the Church, wishing to restore the old Catholic religion.

When she died in 1558, her sister, Queen Elizabeth I of England, did her best to continue their father's work, and turned again to Protestantism. Whilst all the religious changes were being made, something else took place: Wales was gradually growing richer and the people were becoming wealthy from farming and cattle herding. Trade and industry also continued to grow and exports of wool and woollen cloth increased. The Welsh iron and coal industries also grew.

In 1642, the First Civil War broke out between King Charles I of England and Parliament. The war was the product of political manoeuvrings and power struggles. Wales was largely Royalist, apart from the town of Pembroke, which was unswerving in its loyalty to Parliament throughout the war. Many Welsh soldiers were conscripted, and volunteered to fight in the King's Army. However, in 1644 it became clear that the king was losing the war. In September of that year, the Royalists were badly defeated at the Battle of Montgomery. In 1645, the parliamentary army captured North Wales.

At the end of the First Civil War, the north of Wales was still loyal to the king, but in 1646 parliamentary soldiers took control, town by town, finishing in that great site of Welsh battles, Harlech, which was captured on 7 March 1647.

In 1648, Parliament took the decision to disband its army. However, many hadn't been paid and a rebellion took place in Pembroke. Soldiers were sent to Wales and the rebellion was crushed. King Charles I was found guilty of being a 'tyrant, traitor, murderer and public enemy' and was beheaded in Whitehall, London, on 30 January 1649.

Change occurred in Wales with the growth of the Nonconformist church and the eighteenth century saw education being made available to many more children and young people, and not just the ruling classes. In 1761, it is estimated that almost a quarter of a million Welsh people had learned to read and write in schools throughout Wales. The end of the eighteenth century saw the small beginnings of the Industrial Revolution in Wales. The presence of rich mineral resources and a skilled workforce meant the area soon became very different.

THE INDUSTRIAL REVOLUTION IN WALES (1730-1850)

South Wales had long been admired for its natural beauty, but exploitation in the name of Britain's Industrial Revolution changed this forever. Welsh coal had been known about since Roman times and iron works and lead mines were scattered all over the landscape. However, the increasing demand from Britain and the world meant a great increase in population and a permanent disfiguring of the landscape.

New large factories, run by steam, were replacing the home as the centre for British industry. New machines and working practices meant that fewer people were required for the same amount of work. Britain built bigger and better! Ships, bridges and railways throughout the world owed their existence to the manufacturing activity in Wales. Welsh steam coal became the coal of choice, and coke was needed in substantial quantities for the production of iron.

Even though the workforce was large in Wales, more people were needed as the factories, furnaces and mines expanded. Immigrant workers travelled from all over Britain and beyond to find work. In 1801 the population of Monmouthshire was 45,000; 100 years later it was nearly half a million.

Flashes in the sky from furnaces, the hillsides turning black with waste from the pits, and the rows and rows of terraces covering the valleys were elements of the new reality. The green and peaceful lands of South Wales were a distant memory for many, as the land drove the Industrial Revolution and built the British Empire.

Death and injury were commonplace, and illness and premature death were almost certain, as men, women and children worked together in the heat and dust of the mine and the furnace.

DIC PENDERYN, THE MERTHYR TYDFIL MARTYR

Richard Lewis, or Dic Penderyn, was born in 1808 at Aberavon. He travelled to Merthyr in 1819 when his father found work for them both in the coalmines. Richard was always known as Dic Penderyn after the village of Penderyn near Hirwaun where he lodged. Thanks to the Methodist Sunday School Movement he could read and write and was bilingual.

Following the recession of 1828 conditions in the industrial towns were grim. Wage cuts and wholesale job losses, added to by the burden of debt brought about by the hated 'Truck Shop' system, led to mass poverty and starvation among the working population.

By the summer of 1831 most of South Wales was a cauldron of political and civil unrest. The spark that ignited the conflagration came at Merthyr Tydfil where at a town meeting on 30 May 1831, called originally to discuss parliamentary reform, local feelings were running high and the discussion turned to grievances with the local court system and the recovery of small debts from the working population.

The red flag (the symbol of workers' revolt) was raised and while part of the crowd marched to the next town to seek support, the rest, reported to be mostly women and young unemployed men and boys, marched to the records office and burned all the records of outstanding debts. They then went through the town forcibly repossessing furniture and household goods that had previously been seized by the bailiffs and sold to cover their owners' debts.

Troops of the Argyll and Sutherland Highlanders were sent to put down the rioters. In an ugly confrontation in front of the Castle Hotel, as many as twenty people were shot dead.

It is claimed to be the first time that a red flag was waved as a banner of workers' power. In the aftermath of the disturbance, a twenty-three-year-old miner by the name of Richard Lewis was arrested and imprisoned. It is unclear why he should have been singled out for arrest; Dic was accused of wounding Donald Black, one of the Scottish soldiers, but the evidence against him was slender and Black himself apparently could not identify Dic as his assailant. Nevertheless, at his trial in Cardiff, Dic Penderyn was sentenced to the gallows. A petition of 11,000 names was collected testifying to the innocence of Dic Penderyn but despite pleas from church leaders and respected Welsh figures, Lord Melbourne, the Home Secretary, was unmoved. In Parliament he had advocated severe repression of all popular workers' movements as 'unlawful assemblages of armed individuals' and declared that South Wales was 'the worst and most formidable district in the kingdom.' He wrote to a friend that 'the affair we had there in 1831 was the most like a fight of anything that took place.'

Dic Penderyn was hanged outside Cardiff Prison on the gallows in St Mary's Street, Cardiff, on 13 August 1831.

His last words, now immortalised in poem and song, were '*O Arglwydd, dyma gamwedd.*' 'Oh Lord, here is iniquity.'

Thousands flocked to escort his body to his grave through the Vale of Glamorgan, and listened to a funeral sermon from his brother-in-law Morgan Howells. He was buried in St Mary's churchyard, Port Talbot. A plaque to Dic Penderyn can be found at the entrance to Cardiff Market on St Mary's Street, Cardiff.

Regarded as a martyr, his death further embittered relations between Welsh workers and the authorities, but more trouble was brewing.

In 1840 a government commission found that children as young as six were working underground for as long as twelve hours at a time. The young children were expected to operate the ventilation doors in complete darkness. Women hauled the coal from the coalface to the bottom of the mineshaft, to be lifted hundreds of feet to the light above. Mine owners were forbidden from employing women and children for work underground by law in 1842. This was largely ignored, and as late as 1866 there are records of the death of a woman mineworker.

Back above ground it was as dangerous, with dirty and overcrowded settlements giving rise to illness and disease. In 1849, an outbreak of cholera took 800 lives in Merthyr, Dowlais and Aberdare.

In north-east Wales a greater range of industries had developed, with potteries and cotton mills in addition to the iron and coal. The mountains gave more than coal in the north, with copper, lead and slate added to the products stripped from the geologically diverse and rich country of Wales.

By the late eighteenth century, there were nineteen metal works at Holywell and fourteen potteries at Buckley; Holywell and Mold had cotton mills; lead and coal mines were everywhere.

In 1851, in the heat of industrial change, Wales was the world's second leading industrial nation, behind England. English was seen to be the language of business and Welsh culture and identity was further squeezed. Rich businessmen settled in Wales to exploit the natural resources and the Welsh people.

THE PEOPLE SPEAK – CHARTISM

To this backdrop, a working-class movement for political reform was born. It took its name from the People's Charter of 1838, drafted by the London Working Men's Association. Chartism was the first movement of its kind and consisted of many different groups of people from 'working men's associations' to 'artisan groups', shoemakers, printers and tailors. It started as a moral response to poor and dangerous working conditions. However, in many areas it was responsible for strikes, general strikes and a violent rising.

The People's Charter of 1838

Universal male suffrage
A secret ballot
No property qualification for members of Parliament
Pay for members of Parliament (so poor men could serve)
Constituencies of equal size
Annual elections for Parliament

The Chartists obtained 1.25 million signatures and presented the Charter to the House of Commons in 1839. It was rejected by a vote of 235 to 46. Many of the leaders of the movement were arrested, having called for a general strike.

What happened next is one of the most important events in Welsh, and maybe world, political history.

I PREDICT A RISING...

The Newport Rising was the last large-scale armed rising in mainland Britain, when, on 4 November 1839, up to 5,000 Chartists marched on the town.

Preparation had been taking place for a few months, and a prominent figure in the planning was Newport draper and former Mayor, John Frost, who was one of the leaders of the march. The exact intentions behind the march are not clear, although many Chartists were disillusioned with the pursuit of their aims by peaceful means after the rejection of their petition earlier in the year.

According to the Chartist plan, three columns from three valleys would meet and take control of the town of Newport before dawn. Frost led the column that gathered at Blackwood. William Jones, a watchmaker and political radical, led the detachment from Pontypool. Finally, Zephaniah Williams, a coal-miner and master collier, led the detachment from Nantyglo.

Heavy rainfall caused serious problems for the marchers and they were delayed in arriving at the meeting point that had been agreed previously for the three contingents. After spending most of Sunday night outside in the rain the marchers doubted their chances of success, and some never marched into Newport.

News of the rising reached the authorities quite late, and they rushed to make preparations for what they expected to be a significant riot. The Mayor of Newport, Thomas Phillips, had sworn in 500 special constables and asked for more troops to join the sixty already stationed in Newport. He ordered troops and special constables to take up positions alongside him in the Westgate Hotel in the centre of Newport, where they awaited the arrival of the marchers.

The Chartists became convinced that some of their colleagues had been imprisoned in the Westgate. Filing quickly through the town, thousands of Chartists arrived in the square outside the hotel and a bloody and violent battle ensued. The training of the troops and their superior firepower meant that the Chartists found it difficult to enter the building. After half an hour around twenty of them had been killed by the troops, and maybe fifty were injured.

At this point in the battle, leaderless and in chaos, the Chartists dispersed. The Chartist dead were anonymously buried at night at the church of St Woolos in the town to avoid further gatherings of Chartists at the funerals.

CHARTIST ATTACK ON THE WESTGATE INN, NEWPORT, 1839

Over 200 Chartists were arrested and twenty-one were charged with high treason. The three leaders were found guilty and sentenced at the Shire Hall in Monmouth to be hanged, drawn and quartered. However, after petitioning and a nationwide campaign, their sentences were commuted to transportation for life.

They were transported to Van Diemen's Land in Australia.

Frost was eventually granted a pardon and returned to Britain, but never lived in Newport again. He settled in Bristol and was an active advocate of reform until his death, aged ninety-three, in 1877.

At the time, Chartism was considered dangerous and subversive, but a new Reform Bill was passed in August 1867 that gave the vote to all male heads of households over twenty-one, and all male lodgers paying £10 a year in rent.

Further reform arrived with the Ballot Act in 1872, which ensured that votes could be cast in secret – a key demand of the People's Charter – and in 1884 the Third Reform Act extended the qualification of the 1867 Act to the countryside so that almost two thirds of men had the vote.

Eventually, only one of the Chartists' demands (calling for annual parliamentary elections) had failed to become part of British law. At the time, Chartism may have been judged unsuccessful, but there is no doubt that the movement's campaign for electoral reform played an important role in the development of democracy in the UK.

Towards the end of the nineteenth century Socialism continued to develop in response to the poor working and living conditions. The first Labour Member of Parliament was elected in Merthyr Tydfil. Keir Hardie had gone to work in the mines of Scotland at the age of ten, and had dreamed of a life outside the dark and damp conditions of the pits. He started to associate with the Temperance Movement and the Evangelical Union in Scotland. He became a gifted public speaker and in 1879 he was appointed National Secretary of the National Conference of Miners. His energy was boundless and he called for working people to organise themselves to campaign for better living and working conditions.

In this exciting time in the life of British politics, Hardie was elected as Member of Parliament for the constituency of West Ham South in London in 1892. He stood as a candidate before the birth of the Labour Party. He won and took his seat, although he refused to wear the traditional frock coat and top hat that members wore in Parliament.

In 1893 Hardie and others formed the Independent Labour Party, and after making a speech attacking royalty, he lost his seat. Seven years later, in 1900, he would be elected as the first MP for the newly formed Labour Party representing Merthyr Tydfil and Aberdare in the South Wales coalfield. He represented this constituency for the rest of his life.

In the first decade of the twentieth century, Wales experienced another coal boom, and the population grew significantly once again. The Labour Party replaced the Liberals as the strongest political movement in South

Wales. Initially, the Labour Party advocated home rule for Wales, but slowly came to believe that the economy would be better managed centrally from Westminster, and that devolution would undermine the unity of the British Working Class. This disaffected some members, who believed that independence was an urgent task. Eventually, in 1925, this belief would lead to the establishment of Plaid Cymru, by Saunders Lewis, a Welsh Poet, dramatist and political activist and others.

The First World War and the Depression had a significant effect on the Welsh and Wales. Coal production was at an all-time high in 1913 and throughout the First World War Welsh industry supported the war effort. It was after the war in the early 1920s that the outlook became bleak. Industrial unrest and a bitter strike in 1921 brought about the destruction of the old order. By mid-1925 unemployment among British coalminers had risen from 2 per cent the previous year to 28.5 per cent: the South Wales coalfield, heavily dependent on exports, was worst hit.

The Wall Street Crash, on the other side of the Atlantic in 1929, caused further economic suffering for the Welsh and by 1932 unemployment had reached a staggering 43 per cent. Wales had suffered more than any other nation in the developed world. The knock-on effects were also felt in tinplate production, agriculture, iron and steel work and transport. This devastated the economy and the nation.

The starving and poor Welsh left Wales, reducing the population by almost half a million people, and it was not set to recover until the mid-1970s. Unemployment and economic depression continued throughout the 1930s: in 1939, just before the start of the Second World War, unemployment was still 15 per cent.

WAR AND WALES

Wales at war was fully employed. Women entered the industrial workforce in significant numbers once again, and more went to England to work in the factories. The role of the Welsh 'Mam' changed, as women drove buses, lorries and ambulances, and carried out maintenance on aircraft and other industrial tasks. Women were also responsible for heavy agricultural work. The Land Army girls dressed in green, and kept farms and smallholdings running to feed the nation.

Household incomes improved and the arrival of evacuees from the cities increased the population by almost a quarter of a million people.

The people of Wales were determined that when the war eventually finished, they wouldn't return to the austerity and depression they felt between the wars. The Labour

Party, led by Clement Atlee, experienced a tremendous victory in 1945; the people of Wales were looking for a brighter future. In the previous few decades, the economy had collapsed, however, there was change in the air.

A BRIGHT NEW FUTURE?

The transformation that Wales had started to experience during the Second World War continued afterwards too. Unemployment in Wales had disappeared because around 50 per cent of the Welsh workforce was either in the armed forces, or working to support the war effort.

The introduction of the Welfare State, started by Welshman Lloyd George in 1908, was continued by two other Welshmen, who completed the reforms after 1945. James Griffiths and Aneurin (*Nye*) Bevan brought to law the National Insurance Act of 1946. This required all workers to insure themselves against ill health and unemployment. The Industrial Injuries Act of 1948, which ensured that employees injured in the course of their work would be entitled to compensation and a pension, followed this.

1948 also saw the birth of the National Health Service, providing free medical care and prescriptions, glasses and false teeth to all who needed them!

'The verb is more important than the noun'
                                          Aneurin Bevan

The Distribution of Industry Act allowed the use of old heavy industry sites to be redeveloped to create jobs, and government grants were awarded to start new businesses. The nationalisation of some industries and services started in 1947 and a new era began. Coal was still the largest industry in Wales, although the numbers employed fell drastically over the next few years.

The establishment of the 1948 Council of Wales brought back the issue of regional identity, and would advise government on policies for Wales, even though it had no powers. This was the forerunner to the 1951 appointment of a Minister for Welsh Affairs, and the Welsh Office.

The new language of national identity, and a drive to build a future after the terrible years of war and austerity, were among the factors which allowed Plaid Cymru to gain a respectable vote in the general election of 1959, in which the party contested 55 per cent of the country's constituencies, compared with the 7 per cent of Scottish constituencies contested by the Scottish National Party. The Labour Party was surprised at the feeling amongst the voters and redrafted policies.

Partly in order to stave off the nationalist challenge, the 1964 Labour government established the Welsh Office and appointed a Secretary of State for Wales, thus creating a new context for discussion of the government of Wales.

However, Plaid Cymru made a crucial breakthrough in 1966 when the party's president, Gwynfor Evans, was victorious in the Carmarthen by-election. There were further advances from 1974 onwards, and by 1992 Plaid Cymru held four of the forty constituencies of Wales. Such was the feeling that Wales should take steps to rediscover its identity, lost generations before.

When Britain became a member of the European Economic Community in 1972, there were hopes that one day there might be an elected assembly or parliament for Wales. A Royal Commission, a few years later in 1976, recommended sweeping changes in the Wales Bill, although there was no suggestion of any powers being devolved to Wales.

Things were changing in Wales, and they would never be the same. By the late 1970s there was only one colliery left in the Rhondda Valley, a place that had produced coal for well over 100 years.

By 1978, the number of men working in the pits was only 38,000, and by the end of the 1980s it had fallen to fewer than 4,000. The government's intention to close a large proportion of the industry, and modernize by mechanizing and centralizing the rest, was ruthlessly carried out.

Industrial unrest hit a high when the right-wing Conservative Thatcher government announced the closure of twenty mines, and the loss of 20,000 jobs. A national strike was called. Margaret Thatcher increased the pressure by referring to striking miners as 'the enemy within', and continually referred to the action as 'the rule of the mob'.

Arthur Scargill, the President of the National Union of Mineworkers, in turn compared the government's techniques in crowd control to those of a 'Latin American state'. The dispute had little chance of ending amicably or quickly.

Observance of the strike within Wales differed from north to south. In the north, only 35 per cent of the 1,000 men employed went on strike, and this had dwindled to 10 per cent by the strike's end in 1985.

By contrast, the South Wales coalfield contained the staunchest supporters of industrial action. At the start of the strike, 99.6 per cent of the 21,500 workers joined the action. This reduced to 93 per cent by the end. No other area retained such a level. Wales suffered significantly through community breakdown, a rise in deprivation and other effects that are visible to this day.

In other industries, such as tinplate and steel, similar wholesale reorganisation was taking place. The changes in the steel industry resulted in an increase in production, with three new plants being built at Shotton, Margam and Ebbw Vale. Together, these plants produced over a quarter of Britain's total steel production. Milford Haven significantly increased in size as a port and oil refinery and on Anglesey and in the mountains of North Wales nuclear power stations appeared, as well as hydroelectric schemes. In forty years, the economy of Wales had changed significantly; this had an effect on the people who felt they had lost their sense of place, as work, pastimes and recreation took them away from their communities.

A NEW NATION?

During the 1980s and 1990s the question of a National Assembly arose again. In 1979 a referendum had taken place that required 40 per cent of the electorate of Wales to vote in favour for devolution to occur. The disinterest of Labour politicians meant that only 25 per cent eventually voted for the proposal to create an assembly.

However, in 1997 another referendum took place, and this time voters approved the creation of the National Assembly for Wales by a slim majority of 6,712, or 50.3 per cent of the vote. The following year the Government of Wales Act was passed, establishing the Assembly. The new body took over the administrative powers of the Welsh Office, although it had no ability to create legislation itself.

The twentieth century ended with the opening of the Welsh Assembly in Cardiff Bay.

In July 2002, the government established an independent commission to review the powers of the Assembly. The Richard Commission reported in March 2004, and recommended that the National Assembly should have the

power to legislate in certain areas, whilst other area should remain with Westminster. In response the UK government published a report on 15 June 2005, followed by the Government of Wales Act 2006, establishing a parliamentary-type structure, and new powers for the Welsh Government.

Although Plaid Cymru criticised the Act for not delivering a full Welsh Parliament, it was the most significant change in the governance of Wales for 400 years.

Most recently, following a referendum on 3 March 2011, the Welsh Government gained direct law-making powers, without the need to refer matters to Westminster.

The story of Wales continues...

FACTS ABOUT WALES THAT DON'T INVOLVE CASTLES, RUGBY OR DAFFODILS

According to a poll conducted in 2002, Llanddarog in Carmarthenshire is the 'friendliest place' in Wales. Swansea was declared the 'friendliest City in Wales' and the 'second friendliest in the UK', in a survey in 2010.

The Severn Tunnel, which links south Gloucestershire to South Wales, running under the estuary of the River Severn, was the world's longest undersea tunnel for well over 100 years. It was built between 1873 and 1886 and is 4 miles 624 yards long (7km), although only 2.25 miles (3.62km) are underneath the river. Seventy-six million bricks were used in its construction and water needs to be continually pumped out of the tunnel to stop it flooding. Up to 200 trains a day use the tunnel.

The number of coal-miners in Wales peaked at almost 275,000 in 1920; with their families, they accounted for a third of the whole population of Wales

St David's is the least populated city in the UK, with a population of less than 1,500. It is located on the western coast of the Pembrokeshire Coast National Park, and was granted city status because of the presence of a cathedral.

The longest corridor in Europe is to be found in Llandough Hospital near Cardiff. The hospital was opened in 1934, and has been extended considerably. The main corridor is now around 1 mile in length.

The popular image of Welsh 'national' dress is a woman in a red cloak and tall black hat. This image was mostly developed in the nineteenth century. During the revival of Welsh culture and identity, it was felt that traditional values were under threat. The costume regarded as national dress is based on clothing worn by Welsh countrywomen during the early nineteenth century, which was a striped flannel petticoat, worn under a flannel open-fronted bed-gown, with an apron, shawl and kerchief or cap. Styles of bed-gown varied, with loose coat-like gowns, gowns with a fitted bodice and long skirts and also the short gown, which was very similar to a riding habit style. The hats generally worn were the same as hats worn by men at the period. The tall 'chimney' hat did not appear until the late 1840s and seems to be based on an amalgamation of men's top hats and a form of high hat worn during the 1790-1820 period in country areas.

Spiller's record shop in Cardiff is the oldest in the world. It was opened in 1894 by Henry Spiller.

The English are Wales' largest ethnic minority community with 20.3 per cent of the country's population having been born in England.

In 2003, Wales became the first country in the UK in which the majority of babies – 50.3 per cent – were born outside marriage.

In March 1807, the Mumbles to Swansea railway started to carry paying passengers. It had previously been used exclusively for carrying goods to the city docks. In 1870, the horses that pulled the carriages were replaced by a steam locomotive, and in 1929 the railway changed to run on electricity. When it closed in 1960, it was the longest surviving railway in the world.

The smallest house in Britain is in Wales. The Quay House in Conwy is 10ft long and 6ft wide (3.05m x 1.8m). Although it is no longer lived in, the last occupant was Robert Jones, a fisherman who was 6ft 3in (1.9m) tall.

Cardiff only became the capital of Wales in 1955.

The first-ever British newsreel was filmed in Cardiff; it shows the Prince and Princess of Wales attending an exhibition in 1896.

The 'Ugly House' is in Wales, on the A5 between Bettws y Coed and Capel Curig, in the Snowdonia National Park. The 'Ugly House' (*Ty Hyllt*) was built around 1475, when the law allowed for a house to be built almost anywhere, as long as it was completed in one day, between sunrise and sunset. The house was required to have a fireplace and smoke coming out of the chimney when the sun went down. Using rough, undressed stone, the story is that four local brothers completed the mammoth task, and were allowed to keep not only the stone, but also the land surrounding the house, as far as one of them could throw an axe.

A Welshman was responsible for bringing an end to capital punishment in the UK. In February 1956, Parliament voted to abolish the death penalty – even set against the backdrop of rising murder rates throughout the whole of the UK. A book written by a criminal lawyer, Michael Eddowes, had thrown doubt upon the prosecution and subsequent execution of a Welshman called Timothy Evans in 1950. Evans had moved to London with his wife and daughter to find a new life, away from his home in Merthyr, and he sought lodgings at 10 Rillington Place, the home of the infamous serial killer John Reginald Christie. When the bodies of Evans' wife and daughter were found, he was convicted and hanged, and Christie even gave evidence at the trial. He then went on to murder four more women before he was caught. The death penalty was suspended in 1965.

The world's largest second-hand bookshop is in Wales. The town of Hay-on-Wye is Wales' self-styled *Town of Books*.

The otherwise quiet and beautiful border town is a popular destination for those who love books. It's a bibliophile's dream! The town started its love affair with books when resident Richard Booth opened an antique shop which also sold some rare and antiquarian books. He was so successful that soon he was able to open many other shops, including the Old Cinema. Once a year the Hay Literature Festival, which Booth started in 1989, attracts tens of thousands of people who arrive for a week and a half of talks, presentations, concerts, discussions and food and drink.

4

100
WELSH HEROES

In response to the BBC's 2002 opinion poll *100 Greatest Britons*, the *100 Welsh Heroes* poll was run by Culturenet Cymru, a body based at the National Library of Wales in Aberystwyth. It was the largest online poll ever produced, and received nearly 82,000 nominations.

As voted by the people! Here they are:

1. *Aneurin Bevan (2,426 votes)*
Aneurin 'Nye' Bevan (1897-1960) was 45th in the list of the *100 Greatest Britons* and took 1st place in the *100 Welsh Heroes* poll. Nye Bevan was a Welsh Labour politician who was deputy leader of the party from 1959 until his death in 1960. A lifelong campaigner for social justice and champion of the poor, he represented Ebbw Vale for thirty-one years as their Member of

Parliament. He is remembered for his work in establishing the National Health Service, providing free medical care to all in need.

2. *Owain Glyndŵr (2,309 votes)*

Owain Glyndŵr (1349-1416?) was a nobleman, lawyer and soldier, descended from several of the ancient families of Wales. He was declared Prince of Wales, and drew Wales together in a search for freedom and peace in violent times. The King of England responded with military might. However, this wasn't a match for the military tactics of the stealthy forces of Glyndŵr. By 1404, Glyndŵr ruled most of Wales. When his alliances with the French failed, he evaded capture for one last time, probably living out his life on the borders with his daughter and her family.

3. *Tom Jones (2,072 votes)*

Born Thomas John Woodward in Treforest, Pontypridd, in 1940, this gravelly-voiced sex-bomb had a shaky start to his musical career when the BBC banned him after just two singles for being 'too hot to handle'. His notable songs include 'It's Not Unusual', 'Delilah', 'Green, Green Grass of Home' and 'Sex-Bomb'. To date, he has sold over 100 million records and has had thirty-six top 40 hits in the UK and nineteen in the United States. He received an OBE in 1999, then a knighthood from Queen Elizabeth II for his 'services to music' in 2006. Sir Tom's songs can be heard at closing time in almost any Welsh village, town or city, as the appreciative Welsh make their way home, singing any one of his string of hits. One of Wales' greatest exports, *Jones the Voice* has spent almost fifty years delighting audiences from Cwmtillery to Caesar's Palace.

4. *Gwynfor Evans (1,928 votes)*

Dr Richard Gwynfor Evans (1912-2005) was a Welsh politician, lawyer and author, and President of the Welsh political party Plaid Cymru for thirty-six years, being their first MP, elected to Parliament first in 1966. A pacifist and Christian, he is credited with keeping the party going through the difficult post-war years, and bringing them to electoral success. On his death in 2005, Welsh politicians from all parties paid him tribute. In Martin Kettle's commentary on the life and times of Gwynfor Evans, he writes:

> In some circles – though not many of them outside Wales, it must be said – Gwynfor (always Gwynfor, never just Evans) is revered in a way that comes to few public figures. To the faithful, he is something of a saint, spoken of as almost a Welsh Gandhi, a Welsh Martin Luther King, a Welsh Mandela, even a Welsh Mother Theresa. In such circles, Gwynfor is (and was) a man who could, literally, do no wrong.

5. *Richard Burton (1,755 votes)*
Richard Burton CBE (1925-1984) was once the highest paid actor in Hollywood. Originally from Pontrydyfen, he was nominated for seven Academy Awards, but surprisingly never won one. His lack of Oscars didn't seem to diminish the stature of this movie giant, who will always be remembered for his roles in *Look Back in Anger* (1958), *The Spy Who Came in From the Cold* (1965), *Where Eagles Dare* (1968), *Nineteen Eighty-Four* (1984), and of course, as Mark Anthony to Elizabeth Taylor's *Cleopatra* (1963). He is described as 'one of the finest actors of his generation'. Burton once said, 'The Welsh are all actors. It's only the bad ones who become professional.'

6. *Gareth Edwards (1,685 votes)*
Gareth Owen Edwards CBE was born in 1947 and is a former Welsh Rugby union player. He has been described by the BBC as 'arguably the greatest player ever to don a Welsh jersey', winning fifty-three caps playing for Wales and another ten for the British Lions. Former English Rugby team captain Will Carling, in his list of the top 100 rugby players of all time, published in the *Telegraph*

in 2006, places Edwards at number one. 'It's hard to compare generations, yet Edwards is the one guy I can say that would have been great whenever he played. He was a supreme athlete with supreme skills, the complete package. He played in the 1970s, but, if he played now, he would still be the best. He was outstanding at running, passing, kicking and reading the game. He sits astride the whole of rugby as the ultimate athlete on the pitch.'

7. *Dylan Thomas (1,630 votes)*
Dylan Marlis Thomas (1914-1953) was born in Uplands, Swansea. In school it is said that he was an 'undistinguished' student although he went on to write many great poems, including 'Fern Hill', 'Do Not Go Gentle into that Good Night', and 'Death Shall Have no Dominion'. His plays include his famous 'play for voices' *Under Milk Wood* and the collection of stories *Portrait of the Artist as a Young Dog*. Swansea's Dylan Thomas Centre holds a festival each year celebrating Swansea's most famous son, whilst also promoting talent from Wales and beyond.

8. *David Lloyd George (1,627 votes)*
David Lloyd George, 1st Earl Lloyd-George of Dwyfor (1863-1945), was a Liberal politician and statesman, leading the Liberal Party and becoming Chancellor of the Exchequer and Prime Minister. He was also the only Prime Minister to have Welsh as a first language and English second. His leadership in the First World War, and his part in founding the Welfare State, lead many political commentators to state that he was one of the greatest statesmen of the early twentieth century.

9. *Robert Owen (1,621 votes)*
Robert Owen (1771-1858) was born in Newtown, a small market town in mid-Wales in 1771. His father was a saddler and ironmonger in the town. In 1787, Owen moved to London, then to Manchester to work in drapery

shops. At the young age of twenty-one he became a mill manager in the Chorlton Twist Mills, and in his spare time became a social and philosophical reformer, becoming involved with initiatives to improve health and working conditions for factory workers. Moving to New Lanark, Scotland, he married and continued his work there. The living conditions were very harsh, and Owen opened a shop that sold goods for a reasonable price to the workers. He also opened the first infant school in the UK in 1816, developing a *model community* there, believing that life should be more than just work, and that society should be happy and in harmony. He is remembered as a Utopian Socialist and a forerunner of the cooperative movement.

10. *John Saunders Lewis (1,601 votes)*
John Saunders Lewis (1893-1985) was a poet, historian, dramatist and political activist. In 1925, he joined other nationalists at the national eisteddfod, and Plaid Cymru was established. A prolific character in Welsh cultural life, he wrote plays, articles, essays and two novels. He was also nominated for the Nobel Prize for Literature. In 1962, Lewis gave a lecture on BBC radio entitled *Tynged Yr Iaith* (The Fate of the Language). In the speech Lewis predicted the extinction of the Welsh language. As a result of his impassioned lecture the *Cymdeithias yr Iaith Gymraeg* (the Welsh Language Society) was founded.

11. *Mike Peters (1,594 votes)*
Michael Leslie Peters was born in 1959 in Prestatyn, North Wales. The frontman of the Rock New Wave band The Alarm until their split in 1991, he is now a solo artist. He names Woodie Guthrie and David Bowie as influences. His own experiences of suffering with cancer led him to create the Love Hope Strength foundation, raising awareness and money to help those affected by cancer.

12. *Bertrand Russell (1,469 votes)*

Bertrand Arthur William Russell, the 3rd Earl Russell (1872-1970), was born in Trellech. A man of many talents, he was a philosopher, logician, mathematician, historian and social critic. As a prominent anti-war activist he was sent to prison during the First World War. Later he campaigned against Adolf Hitler, Stalin and the United States of America's involvement in Vietnam. He was awarded the Nobel Prize for Literature in 1950 for his significant writings in 'Humanitarian ideals and freedom of thought'.

13. *Catherine Zeta-Jones (1,136 votes)*

Darling of the silver screen, Catherine Zeta-Jones CBE was born in Swansea in 1969. She won an Academy Award for Best Supporting Actress for her role in the 2002 adaptation of the musical *Chicago*, plus several other significant awards. She is married to the actor Michael Douglas and they have two children, their son Dylan Michael Douglas being named after Dylan Thomas, No. 7 in this list.

14. *R.S. Thomas (898 votes)*

The Welsh poet and Anglican priest Ronald Stuart Thomas (1913-2000) was born in Cardiff. In *The Guardian* just after his death, Byron Rogers wrote:

He was the strangest bundle of contradictions. This was the poet who wrote, of country clergymen, that they were *'Toppled into the same graves with oafs and yokels,'* but was a country clergyman himself, the oafs and yokels the ancestors of his own parishioners.

The contradictions in his role as a clergyman weren't the only ones in his work: his poem 'A Priest to His People' starts:

Men of the hills, wantoners, men of Wales / With your sheep and your pigs and your ponies, your sweaty females, how I have hated you...

All this from the man who wrote that he was such an extreme nationalist he could not support Plaid Cymru because it recognised the English Parliament. Nevertheless, Thomas himself said that there was a 'lack of love for human beings' in his poetry. However, people still loved his poetry; his final works would sell over 20,000 copies in the UK alone.

15. *Andrew Vicari (873 votes)*
Andrew Vicari was born in Port Talbot in 1938 was called the 'King of Painters' in *Paris Match* magazine. As a child he wanted to become a painter, and won £10 in a local competition and went on to become the youngest ever student at the famous Slade School in London. Following in the footsteps of Holbein and Van Dyck he has accepted patronage from the rich of the day. He has painted commissions for the King and Government of Saudi Arabia, where there are three museums full of his work. He has had his work displayed in China, and has recently bought Picasso's old villa, planning to turn it into an art school.

16. *Evan Roberts (816 votes)*   .
Evan Roberts (1878-1951) was raised a Calvinistic Methodist, and in 1904 began studying for Christian ministry at Newcastle Emlyn. Roberts began a series of meetings to bring about Revival in the Christian church, and was instrumental in the Great Revival of 1904-1905, one of the most dramatic events in Wales in terms of the effect on the population, and its repercussions beyond Wales.

17. *James Dean Bradfield (790 votes)*
Born on 21 February 1969 in Pontypool, Bradfield is the lead guitarist and vocalist for the Welsh rock band Manic Street Preachers, which he formed with his cousin Sean Moore and two other close friends Nicky Wire and Richey James Edwards. Bradfield is quoted as saying:

We were all born within a mile of each other. All born in the same town. So we've always shared the same influences, the same language, basically, and that makes us very close. There's no ego involved. When we formed the band, it wasn't like, oh, I want to be the singer, or I want to be the guitarist, or I want to write the lyrics, we just found what we could do, we found what we were best at.

Bradfield has enjoyed success with the Manic Street Preachers, but also as a solo artist.

18. *Bishop William Morgan (775 votes)*

William Morgan (1544-1604) was born in Ty Mawr Wybrnant, near Betws-y-Coed. He was educated by the chaplain of a wealthy local family, and probably went to Westminster School for a time before going up to St John's College, Cambridge. He was a passionate theologian and became the university's preacher in 1575. He returned to Wales to take up several parishes and started to translate the Bible into Welsh, believing that there was a great need

for the people to read the scriptures in their own language. His early translation was commended by several people, including Owain Gwynedd and Ieuan Tew.

In 1547, however, the Act of Uniformity was passed in the time of Edward VI (although the king was only nine at the time). His protectors insisted that all public services in England and Wales would be held in English, and not Latin or any other language, and it seemed that the Welsh language would die out. However, in 1563 Elizabeth I passed an Act ordering the translation of the Bible and the Book of Common Prayer into Welsh. Eventually, Morgan completed and revised his earlier works, and both Old and New Testaments were widely published in 1588.

In 1595, Morgan was appointed the Bishop of Llandaff, then Bishop of St Asaph in 1601. Richard Parry and Dr John Davies completed a new translation he was working on when he died in 1604; this became the standard Welsh Bible until the twentieth century and continues to be used to this day. His achievement is now considered to be a major event in the history of the Welsh language.

19. *John Charles (769 votes)*
William John Charles CBE (1931-2004), born in Swansea, was a Welsh international footballer and is considered by many to have been the greatest all-round British footballer. Whether centre-half or centre forward, he was world class in both positions. He could also have played fullback or midfield if required. This versatility meant that he managed to break the Leeds United Football Club scoring a record of forty-two goals in a season, at the same time as appearing as centre-half for Wales. In his first game as captain for the Welsh team in 1957, he was spotted by Umberto Agnelli, President of the Italian football team Juventus, at the game. He was eventually signed for £65,000, a record transfer fee for a British player. He continued scoring goals at an alarming rate, attracting even greater transfer fees each time he moved clubs. He eventually retired in 1966, having played thirty-eight games for Wales. Drifting in and out of football, he tried his hand as a publican and shopkeeper. He will be remembered for being a gentle giant, never being sent off or cautioned, and arguably the finest player to represent Wales in football.

20. *Phil Campbell (763 votes)*

Philip Anthony *Wizzö* Campbell, born in Pontypridd in 1961, has been the lead guitarist of Motörhead, the British heavy metal band, since 1983. Even though the band tour extensively throughout the world, and his fellow band members live in Los Angeles and Gothenburg, he continues to live in Pontypridd with his wife Gaynor, and their children Todd, Dane and Tyla.

21. *Llywelyn ap Gruffudd (564 votes)*

Llywelyn ap Gruffudd or *Llywelyn the Last* (1223-1282), was the last prince of an independent Wales. On 21 March 1282, Llywelyn's brother, Dafydd, attacked Hawarden Castle and sparked off the war of 1282-83. Llywelyn was faced with an almost impossible dilemma. Torn between his agreement with the king and his loyalty to his brother and his people, Llywelyn sided with his brother and led the Welsh resistance to the inevitable invasion by Edward I. By the end of the year Llywelyn was dead, having been killed on 11 December in a brief engagement with English forces at Irfon Bridge near Builth Wells.

22.   *Ioan Gruffudd (464 votes)*

Ioan Gruffudd was born in Llwydcoed, in 1973. Training as an actor at the Royal Academy of Dramatic Art, he rose to prominence in roles in the films *Titanic*, *Black Hawk Down* and *102 Dalmatians*. He is also well known for playing Horatio Hornblower in *Hornblower*, the adaptations of the C.S. Forrester novels. A versatile actor, Gruffudd has also played William Wilberforce in the historical drama *Amazing Grace*, and ex-British Prime Minister Tony Blair in a biopic. A Welsh speaker, Gruffudd has been inducted into the *Gorsedd Beirdd Ynys Prydain* (the Bardic Order of Great Britain) and promotes Welsh language television coverage wherever possible.

23. *Richey Edwards (436 votes)*

Richard James Edwards, born in 1967, was a member of the Welsh band the Manic Street Preachers from its formation in 1986 until he disappeared on 1 February 1995. After appearing on the BBC music show *Top of the Pops* controversially dressed in army uniforms, the band was told by the BBC that they had received 'the most complaints ever'. Shortly after, Edwards disappeared from the Embassy Hotel in London on 1 February 1995. His car was found abandoned on 17 February near the Severn View service station, near the Severn Bridge. A police search of the car confirmed that it had been lived in for a few days. Edwards was never seen again. In November 2008 his family declared him presumed dead. He was known for his intellectual and political lyrics, and has been described as an eloquent character. In 2009, the ninth Manic Street Preachers album *Journal for Plague Lovers* was released, composed entirely of lyrics left behind by Edwards.

24. *J.P.R. Williams (433 votes)*

John Peter Rhys Williams, born in 1949 in Cardiff, is one of the Welsh rugby greats, who during the 1970s was an aggressive, attacking full-back, and who with his long side-burns and socks around his ankles was one of the most recognisable figures in Welsh sport. With awesomely efficient defence, he was a formidable tackler, appearing as if out of nowhere to rescue difficult situations. Between 1969 and 1981, JPR helped Wales win six Triple Crowns and three Grand Slams. Not many people know that in 1966 JPR won junior Wimbledon and in an interview with *The Guardian* in 2008 he said that he would have 'chosen tennis before rugby' if he were to make the same decision today, because of the 'dangers of rugby, it's much more physical than when I played'. JPR lives now in the Vale of Glamorgan, having retired from being an orthopaedic surgeon.

25. *Tanni Grey-Thompson (432 votes)*
Baroness Tanni Grey-Thompson was born in Cardiff in 1969 and is considered to be one of the most successful Paralympic athletes ever. Her career started in the 100 metres at the Junior National Games for Wales in 1984. Her international career began in 1988 at the Seoul Olympics, where she won a bronze medal in the 400 metres. At her fifth and last Paralympic games in 2004 in Athens, she won two gold medals. As a paralympian, she has won sixteen medals; eleven gold, four silver and a bronze. She also holds thirteen World Championship medals; six gold, five silver and two bronze. A television presenter and charity trustee, she was made a Life Peer on the recommendation of the House of Lords in 2010; she sits as a crossbencher.

So, what about the rest?

26. *Simon Weston (416 votes)* – War hero of the Falklands War
27. *John Evans (352 votes)* – Writer and filmmaker
28. *Alfred Russell Wallace (313 votes)* – Naturalist and explorer
29. *Michael D. Jones (284 votes)* – Founder of Welsh Patagonia
30. *Dafydd ap Gwilym (281 votes)* – Poet
31. *Archbishop Rowan Williams (273 votes)* – Former Archbishop of Canterbury
32. *Patrick Jones (260 votes)* – Poet, playwright and filmmaker
33. *Cayo Evans (257 votes)* – Political activist
34. *Tommy Cooper (219 votes)* – Comedian
35. *Roald Dahl (201 votes)* – Author
36. *John Frost (187 votes)* – Chartist leader
37. *Hedd Wyn (178 votes)* – Poet
38. *Jimmy Wilde (177 votes)* – Boxer
39. *Dr Richard Price (171 votes)* – Philosopher

40. *Sir Kyffin Williams (170 votes)* – Artist
41. *Kate Roberts (167 votes)* – Writer
42. *Roy Jenkins (165 votes)* – Politician
43. *Hywel Dda (164 votes)* – King and lawgiver
44. *Anthony Hopkins (160 votes)* – Actor
45. *Professor Steve Jones (159 votes)* – Biologist
46. *Saint David (158 votes)* – Patron Saint of Wales
47. *William Williams Pantycelyn (158 votes)* – Poet and hymn writer
48. *Donald Davies (146 votes)* – Scientist
49. *Ron Davies (145 votes)* – Politician
50. *Professor Brian Josephson (144 votes)* – Scientist
51. *Sir Henry Morton Stanley (143 votes)* – Explorer
52. *T.E. Lawrence (143 votes)* – War hero and author
53. *Henry Tudor (VII) (142 votes)* – King of England
54. *Llywelyn ab Iorwerth (139 votes)* – Prince of Wales
55. *Bryn Terfel (138 votes)* – Singer
56. *Dic Penderyn (136 votes)* – Political martyr
57. *Ian Rush (135 votes)* – Footballer
58. *Neil Kinnock (135 votes)* – Politician
59. *W.H. Davies (135 votes)* – Poet
60. *Mark Hughes (132 votes)* – Footballer
61. *Sir Clough William-Ellis (120 votes)* – Architect
62. *Bill Frost (120 votes)* – Aviator
63. *Dafydd Iwan (115 votes)* – Musician and politician
64. *Dr William Price (114 votes)* – Physician and eccentric
65. *Elizabeth Phillips Hughes (110 votes)* – Educator
66. *Margaret Haig Thomas (108 votes)* – Suffragette
67. *Professor Clive Granger (107 votes)* – Economist
68. *Terry Matthews (95 votes)* – Entrepreneur
69. *Howell Harris (94 votes)* – Religious leader
70. *King Arthur (92 votes)* – King of the Britons
71. *Cerys Matthews (88 votes)* – Singer
72. *Laura Ashley (87 votes)* – Designer
73. *William Henry Preece (86 votes)* – Inventor and Engineer
74. *David Davies (81 votes)* – Industrialist
75. *Thomas Jones (81 votes)* – Artist

76. *Colin Jackson (77 votes)* – Athlete
77. *Captain Henry Morgan (71 votes)* – Buccaneer
78. *Julian MacDonald (68 votes)* – Fashion Designer
79. *Gwen John (68 votes)* – Artist
80. *Rhodri Mawr (64 votes)* – King
81. *Iolo Morganwg (63 votes)* – Poet and author
82. *Alexander Cordell (63 votes)* – Author
83. *Owain Lawgoch (62 votes)* – Claimant to the Welsh Throne
84. *Dannie Abse (62 votes)* – Poet
85. *Gerald of Wales (60 votes)* – Bishop and writer
86. *Robert Recorde (57 votes)* – Mathematician
87. *David Edward Hughes (57 votes)* – Scientist and musician
88. *Richard Amerik (57 votes)* – Customs officer, sheriff and merchant
89. *Evan [Ieuan Fardd] Evans (57 votes)* – Poet
90. *Richard Wilson (56 votes)* – Artist
91. *William Grove (56 votes)* – Judge and scientist
92. *Megan Lloyd George (56 votes)* – Politician
93. *John Jones (55 votes)* – Astronomer
94. *Raymond Williams (55 votes)* – Writer
95. *John Cale (55 votes)* – Musician
96. *Ernest Jones (54 votes)* – Psychiatrist
97. *Waldo Williams (53 votes)* – Poet
98. *The Lord Rhys (51 votes)* – Prince of Deheubarth
99. *Isaac Roberts (44 votes)* – Engineer and businessman
100. *Elizabeth Andrews (37 votes)* – Political activist

SO, WHAT HAPPENED NEXT?

The list of heroes is certainly an exciting journey through Welsh history to the present day; it lists some of Wales' best exports in the fields of science, the arts, politics and religion. It has proved to be controversial, however.

Rumblings that there was a 'Welsh Nationalist' plot to place Owain Glyndŵr at number one were persistent.

There was also a suggestion that a division between Welsh speakers and non-Welsh speakers had arisen. A few months later, there was an allegation that the poll had been 'rigged' to avoid 'dumbing down'. At the height of the controversy, Peter Black, Welsh Assembly Member for South West Wales, called for an inquiry into whether public funds used for the poll were used properly, and whether there should be a refund to the Welsh Assembly Government.

As they say in Wales, *Nid aur yw popeth melyn* / Every yellow thing is not gold.

QUOTES FROM FAMOUS
WELSH PEOPLE ABOUT WALES

Catherine Zeta-Jones, actress

'In Wales it's brilliant. I go to the pub and see everybody who I went to school with. And everybody goes, "So what you doing now?" And I go, "Oh, I'm doing a film with Antonio Banderas and Anthony Hopkins." And they go, "Ooh, good." And that's it.'

Dylan Thomas, poet and writer

'Wales is the land of my fathers. And my fathers can have it.'

'Up through the lubber crust of Wales
I rocketed to astonish
The flashing needle rock of squatters,
The criers of Shabby and Shorten,
The famous stitch droppers.'

Tom Jones, musician

'I haven't become an American! Having a house in LA is just where the house is. It's just a convenience thing living there. I carry Wales around inside me. I'd consider moving back there one day. I never really left.'

Giraldus Cambrensis (1146-1223), clergyman

'Happy and fortunate indeed would this nation be, nay, completely blessed, if it had good prelates and pastors, and but one prince, and that prince a good one.'

'Evil borders upon good, and vices are confounded with virtues; as the report of good qualities is delightful to a well-disposed mind, so the relation of the contrary should not be offensive.'

'Nor do I think that any other nation than this of Wales, nor any other language, whatever may hereafter come to pass, shall on the day of severe examination before the Supreme

Judge, answer for this corner of the earth.'

'No one of this nation ever begs, for the houses of all are common to all; and they consider liberality and hospitality amongst the first virtues.'

'Not addicted to gluttony or drunkenness, this people who incur no expense in food or dress, and whose minds are always bent upon the defence of their country, and on the means of plunder, are wholly employed in the care of their horses and furniture.'

SOME LOVELY WELSH
WORDS AND PHRASES

The phrase for 'tired' is *wedi blino*.

Some difficult ones to pronounce are *llongyfarchiadau* meaning 'congratulations', and *ddiddordebau* meaning 'interests or hobbies'.

In Welsh the phrase for 'please' is *os gwelwch yn dda* and 'thank you' is *diolch yn fawr*.

The Welsh people are *Cymry* and the land is called *Cymru*.

Lloegr is England, and the English people are *Saeson*.

Cymru am byth means 'Wales for ever'.

Bore da is 'good morning'.

Prynhawn da is 'good afternoon'.

Noswaith dda is 'good evening'.

Nos da is 'good night', and

Cwrw Da is 'good beer'.

Hwyl means 'bye'.

Penblwydd hapus means 'happy birthday', and *pob lwc* is 'good luck'.

Cariad is 'love'.

'Hug' is *cwtch* and *Twp* means 'stupid'.

SOME FUNNY SAYINGS
SOMETIMES HEARD IN WALES

Directions and time

'It's a five minute walk if you run.'
'I'll do it now in a minute.'
'It's over by there.'
'Where are you to?'

Parental Advice

'If you fall out of that tree and break your leg, don't come running to me.'
'One of these mornings you'll wake up dead if you're not careful.'

Compliments

'There's nice your hair is.'

And the truly classic...

'Whose coat is that jacket?'

5

VISITORS
TO WALES

Over the centuries, there have been many visitors to Wales. Some have enjoyed the beautiful mountains and beaches; some settled with the people; some have wanted to discover more of the nation. Some visitors wanted to invade and exploit the natural resources. Over the next few pages, we look at some prolific visitors to the Wales down the years.

THE ROMANS: WE CAME, WE SAW, WE BUILT SOME ROADS

Firstly we have the mighty Imperial Roman Army, visitors who made quite an impact on Welsh life, and then almost faded away. It's a bloodthirsty story of invasion and resistance.

When the Roman Army invaded Britain in AD 48, they met formidable opposition when they marched into Wales. Fighting with the Welsh tribes was usually a costly exercise, in terms of losses and morale. The Welsh seemed able to attack with fierce determination, inflict a great deal of damage, and then disappear to regroup in the mountains, hills and forests.

At the time of the invasion, there were five tribes in Wales, who were brought together to fight the Romans by an enigmatic character named Caratacus. He was a veteran of leading the British resistance to the Romans further east. Following a defeat at a battle close to the River Medway, he was driven away from his native lands and fled to Wales, along with the remains of his army.

Leading the border tribes of the Ordovices and the Silures, Caratacus waged a successful guerrilla war against the Romans, which culminated in the Battle of Caer Caradoc, fought in AD 50.

Caratacus chose a battlefield in the hills, placing his troops on higher ground. The approach for the Romans was both difficult and dangerous. Where it was most shallow, he built stone fortifications and placed armed men in front of them.

It is believed that this battle took place on the banks of the River Severn or possibly the Teme. The Roman commander, Publius Ostorius Scapula, was wary about attacking from the front of the battlefield, being concerned that the opposing troops would overpower his soldiers.

As the battle commenced, missiles rained down on the Roman Army, and they employed all their skill in forming the men to avoid serious casualties and deaths. Slowly, they reached the stone ramparts and started to dismantle them. Once inside the defences, the Romans sustained serious losses in the bloody fighting, but their military skill eventually secured the victory. Caratacus's wife, son and daughter were captured, but Caratacus escaped, fleeing north to the Brigantes. The Brigantian queen, however, betrayed him and he was handed over to the Romans in chains.

When he was transported to Rome, Caratacus was exhibited as part of the Emperor Caludius's triumph. He gave a speech, speaking of the valour and courage of his people, and the strength of the Roman Army. Caratacus's courage, even from the jaws of defeat, was celebrated and he and his family were pardoned and freed. The Senators of the day declared the victory as one of Rome's greatest, and the commander, Ostorius Scapula, was awarded triumphal ornaments.

Several years later in AD 61, the Romans attacked the isle of Anglesey, stronghold of the druids, and what was left of the British resistance. The Roman historian Tacitus recorded the approach across the Menai Strait:

> On the coastline, a line of warriors of the opposition was stationed, mainly made up of armed men, amongst them women, with their hair blowing in the wind, while they were carrying torches. Druids were amongst them, shouting terrifying spells, their hands raised towards the heavens, which scared our soldiers so much that their limbs became paralysed. As a result, they remained stationary and were injured. At the end of the battle, the Romans were victorious, and the holy oaks of the druids were destroyed.

It wasn't until around AD 90 that most of the Welsh tribes had been subjugated to Roman rule. A question remains as to whether the whole of Wales was actually occupied by force: a mosaic found in the Forum in Rome suggests that the far north-western corner of Wales, the land of the Ordovices, was never conquered.

As the Romans divided their new province Britannia into lowland and highland zones, three major fortresses were constructed: one to protect the border at York, one at Chester, and another beside the River Usk, which they called Isca Silurum. The bloodthirsty Welsh needed to be subjected to tight military control by means of a network of forts, under the command of not one, but two legions.

Isca Silurum, now known as Caerleon on Usk, became the home of the Second Augustan Legion, and is the most important Roman site in Wales.

Caerleon held a force of around 5,600 men and the town was equipped with all the usual luxuries that the Romans would expect – such as an amphitheatre for gladiatorial battles – while bathhouses and temples were all laid out in the classic Roman plan. Surrounding the fort were several other stations to help protect them, in Abergavenny, Usk, Monmouth, Cardhill, Neath and Loughor. A little further away in mid-Wales, Castle Collen, near Llandrindod Wells, operated as a substantial outpost. The Welsh were controlled by almost thirty auxiliary forts, joined by straight roads, spaced a day's march from each other.

Over the next 100 or so years, the Romans settled into Welsh life, and they relaxed a bit, they farmed and built villas. In the south, tribes were allowed some form of self-government, although in the north there was a greater military presence. They dug for coal, lead, copper, gold and silver; they worshipped Celtic deities alongside their Roman gods, and cultivated large areas of land, especially along the coastal areas of South Wales, where the rich and successful Romans lived.

By the time the Romans left Wales in AD 383, they also left Wales with quite a legacy.

The BBC programme *What the Romans Did for Us* tells us that the Red Dragon *y Ddraig Gogh* that appears on the Welsh flag was of Roman origin, as was the leek a symbol of Wales and the Welsh, and several words in the Welsh language found their way in from the Latin too. For example:

The Welsh word for church, *eglwys*, is from the Latin *ecclesia*
The Welsh word for sausage, *selsig*, is from the Latin *salsica*
The Welsh word for window, *ffesnestr*, is from the Latin *fenestra*
The Welsh word for glove, *maneg*, is from the Latin *manica*

By AD 410, the Romans had left Britain completely. Leaving lovely straight roads and strange buildings with under-floor central heating! They also left some other useful stuff too, like the calendar, coins, turnips and carrots, wine, glass, cabbages and peas, cement and bricks, cats, apples, pears and grapes, public baths and stinging nettles. Phew!

So, who else came to visit Wales?

GEORGE BORROW, VICTORIAN GENTLEMAN

Gentleman writer George Henry Borrow (1803-1881) was born in Norfolk. The son of a militia captain, he moved around with his father's regiment between England, Scotland and Ireland. However, it was as a child on Mousehold Heath, in the hills above Norwich, that he met the gypsies, and was introduced to the Romani language.

Initially, Borrow trained as a solicitor, but his heart wasn't in it. He could speak twelve languages by the age of eighteen. When his father died, he moved to London to find work as an author. This was harder than he had imagined, and he didn't have much luck, so in 1825 he left the city in search of adventure. He became a tinker and an ostler in England, eventually finding himself travelling to the Continent.

Borrow eventually travelled to Russia, Spain, Portugal and Morocco, meeting and mixing with the gypsies, learning more of their language and culture.

He became a bestselling author when his book *The Bible in Spain* (1843) was published. It was an account of five years spent there. He was well regarded and enjoyed a degree of fame, becoming an early modern travel writer.

Returning to England, he settled in Suffolk, marrying a rich widow and writing up the stories of his travels. Travelling around 20 miles a day, never in a straight line, he had seen things that others only dreamed of.

His last major work was *Wild Wales: Its People, Language and Scenery,* which was published in 1862.

Wild Wales recounted Borrow's personal experiences as he toured Wales on foot, after a family holiday in Llangollen in 1854. The book has been described as 'robust, dramatic and cheerful'. Borrow had gone to some lengths to learn Welsh, and although the language was spoken with an East Anglian lilt, it appears he was quite proficient. 'I never heard before of an Englishman speaking Welsh,' said a man in Wrexham. 'Is the gentleman Welsh?' wondered one man near Llangollen; 'he seems to speak Welsh very well.' One hostile Welshman, Borrow noted on the road to Llanfair in Anglesey, was 'confused at hearing an Englishman speak Welsh, a language which the Welsh in general imagine no Englishman can speak, the tongue of an Englishman as they say being not long enough to pronounce Welsh.' None knew quite what to make of him. In the north they mistook him for a South Walian. In the south they assumed he was North Walian.

Borrow gives a detailed account of his travels in Wales, starting in North Wales, travelling through Wrexham, Llangollen, Corwen, Betws-y-Coed to Bangor, then Anglesey and Caernarfon. Finishing his travels in the north in Bala and Machynlleth, he travels through mid-Wales to Tregaron and Lampeter. Then on to the industrial south, through Brynamman, Merthyr Tydfil and Pontardawe. His mammoth journey continues in Neath, Swansea, making his way towards Caerphilly, Newport and Chepstow back to England.

The introduction to *Wild Wales* starts with these words, which set the scene:

WALES is a country interesting in many respects, and deserving of more attention than it has hitherto met with. Though not very extensive, it is one of the most picturesque countries in the world, a country in which Nature displays herself in her wildest, boldest, and occasionally loveliest forms. The inhabitants, who speak an ancient and peculiar language, do not call this region Wales, nor themselves Welsh. They call themselves Cymry or Cumry, and their country Cymru, or the land of the Cumry. Wales or Wallia, however, is the true, proper, and without doubt the original name, as it relates not to any particular race, which at present inhabits it, or may have sojourned in it at any long bygone period, but to the country itself. Wales signifies a land of mountains, of vales, of dingles, chasms, and springs.

When Borrow travelled around Wales he conducted a sort of informal census of the proportion of the local who spoke Welsh. In the north and west, he found more people saying *dim Saesneg*, no English, and just beyond Newport the language disappeared altogether.

Without a doubt, the book *Wild Wales* is a wonderful snapshot of the Welsh, their culture and their concerns, and George Henry Borrow is one of the most interesting visitors Wales has given a welcome to.

THE WYE TOUR –
LONDON, PARIS, ROME, CHEPSTOW

From the 1660s, the traditional Grand Tour of Europe would have taken between several months and several years to complete. Young gentlemen of means travelled to France, Italy, Spain and in later years to Germany and Switzerland with a guide. By the late eighteenth century, young ladies also took the Tour.

Samuel Johnson observed in 1776 that: 'A man who has not been in Italy, is always conscious of an inferiority, from his not having seen what it is expected a man should see.'

The travellers were expected to finish their education with this extensive trip of Europe, experiencing the natural beauty and the cultural treasures.

There were many different routes the young and rich could undertake, but the standard route took the travellers to Paris and the Alps. Some tourists, including Byron, made it as far as Greece. But the must visit destination was Italy, with its Renaissance glories and classical splendours.

The Grand Tour is said to have added considerably to the cultural and artistic wealth of Britain, as the Grand Tourists brought many ideas and concepts back.

Journeys became difficult to schedule, to fit in with the periods of peace between Britain and France. At the end of the Seven Years' War in 1763, there was a new flood of visitors to the Continent. But, in 1796, Napoleon occupied Italy, and it all stopped.

Then something rather curious happened in Wales.

The Wye Tour was a trip along the River Wye, which had been popular for a few years. Visitors enjoyed the natural phenomena, scenic views, historic castles and buildings and even the varied industry along the river. It had been popularised in the mid-eighteenth century after the publication of the not so snappily titled *William Gilpin's Observations of the River Wye and several parts of South Wales, etc. relative chiefly to Picturesque Beauty; made in the Summer of 1770.*

Gilpin was an English artist, Anglican cleric, schoolmaster and author. He coined the aesthetic ideal of something being picturesque, instructing travellers to examine 'the face of the country by the rules of picturesque beauty', along with the cultural strands of Gothic and Celtic artefacts. This appreciation of the beautiful and the sublime was a key factor in the emergence of a Romantic movement at the time.

Travellers from all over Britain were flocking to Ross-on-Wye, on the borders of Wales, to start their tours, sailing downriver to Chepstow, over the course of a few days. During the early nineteenth century, the tours were at the height of their popularity, and not only the rich and well-heeled attended, ensuring the success of the Tour until well after the end of the Napoleonic Wars and the Picturesque Movement.

In 1800 there were eight to ten boats being launched from Ross-on-Wye each day, equipped with drawing tables and travel journals, canopies to protect travellers from the sun and luxurious interiors. At three guineas a day, these boats were not restricted to the super-wealthy, but would have been available to those with more modest incomes also.

Tourists could also walk along the banks of the Wye, appreciating the banks, hills and the bends in the river. Goodrich Castle, set high on a hillside, would appear, with its artefacts of the Civil War, complete with mortar and cannonballs. As the tour continued, the New Weir ironworks and the Simmonds Yat rock, a 470ft (140m) outcrop, would give the tourists a sense of the sublime.

At the end of the day, they would finish their walk or cruise in Monmouth, and enjoy a night in an inn. Early the following morning, the tour would take them through the picturesque countryside of the Welsh borders, until they arrived at the highlight of the tour, one of the greatest sights in Britain, Tintern Abbey. There the tourists would see the ruins of what was once a massive Cistercian

SOME MORE WELSH FACTS

The population of Cardiff in 1801 was 1,870. It is now nearly 350,000.

Buffalo Bill and his Wild West show visited Wales in 1891, 1903 and 1904.

In 2012, in Porthcawl, 814 people turned out dressed as Elvis, setting a new world record for the largest gathering of Elvis Presley impersonators. The existing record was set in Las Vegas in 2012. The attempt was part of the Porthcawl Elvis festival, the biggest event of its kind in Europe.

In the First World War, Cardiff was the largest coal port in the world.

Canada was explored and mapped by the Welsh. John Evans and Meriweather Lewis helped map the North American continent, but another Welshman, David Thompson, was 'the man who measured Canada', covering 80,000 miles on foot, dog sled, horseback and canoe. He detailed the continent in seventy-seven volumes detailing his geographical, biological and ethnographical findings.

6

STOP PRESS: THE WELSH DISCOVERED AMERICA!

Madoc or Madog ab Owain Gwynedd, according to legend, was a Welsh prince who sailed to America in 1170, over 300 years before Christopher Columbus' voyage in 1492.

Madoc was one of the many illegitimate sons of Owain Gwynedd, the most powerful leader in Wales at the time. He was born around Dolwyddelan Castle on the edge

of Snowdonia. When Owain died at the end of 1170, there was violent dispute amongst his sons over the inheritance of the kingdom. To avoid the family feuding, and the war-like conditions that had occurred in Gwynedd due to his father's death, Madoc fled to find exile in the Norse city of Dublin.

The city was famed for shipbuilding and seafaring, and many Welsh had settled there to avoid troubles in Wales. Madoc's brother Rhiryd was Lord of Clochran near Dublin. Although Owain Gwynedd had many illegitimate sons, Madoc and Rhiryd were related not just through their father, but also through their grandmother, Ragnhilde, wife of Gruffyd ap Cynan, the grand-daughter of the Norse king of Dublin, the wonderfully named Sitric Silkenbeard.

Legend has it that Madoc had a ship built, which he called *Gwennan Gorn*, and together with his brother in his own ship the *Pedr Sant*, left from the ancient quay, near a little stream called the Afon Ganol, in Rhos-on-Sea, and sailed out into the wild blue yonder ... to the west.

Madoc is then said to have landed at what is now Point Morgan, Mobile Bay, Alabama. He then left the settlers there and returned to Wales to collect a much larger group of colonists, sailing with them from Lundy Island in the Bristol Channel, intending to start a new life, far from his troubles in Gwynedd.

Madoc's people were said to have moved hundreds of miles inland up the Alabama, Coosa and Ohio rivers. As they travelled they constructed stone forts that the local Cherokee tribes, to this day, claim were constructed by 'white people'. These have been dated to a period several hundred years before the arrival of Colombus, and would fit with the story of Madoc and Rhiryd. The forts are also of a similar design to that of Dolwyddelan Castle in North Wales, the presumed birthplace of Madoc.

At first the settlers fought with the native tribes, but eventually they became part of them. Tales of inter-marriage with the local Native Americans, and tribes of Welsh-speaking Indians are common. There are also stories of Welsh Indians building a number of landmarks that bear similarities to earthworks and monuments in Wales.

The stories of Madoc and Rhiryd were told most commonly during the Elizabethan period when English and Welsh writers wished to prove that North America was the property of the English Crown, but the stories have remained popular ever since. This Tudor political scheming, and the claims about the Welsh in America, has made many historians suspicious about any real link, however there have been claims of further evidence to prove the legend, the most persistent of all Welsh stories.

It is true to say, however, that early pioneers and explorers believed they had found evidence of a Welsh influence. In the eighteenth century, one local tribe, the Mandans, were described as 'white men with forts, towns and permanent villages laid out in streets and squares'. They claimed Welsh ancestry and spoke a very different language to the neighbouring tribes.

Instead of canoes, Mandans fished from coracles, an ancient type of boat still found in Wales today. It was also observed that unlike members of other tribes, these people grew white-haired with age. In addition, in 1799 Governor John Sevier of Tennessee wrote a report in which he mentioned the discovery of six skeletons encased in brass armour bearing the Welsh coat of arms.

In 1953 a plaque was placed in Mobile Bay, which reads: 'In memory of Prince Madog, a Welsh explorer who landed on the shores of Mobile Bay in 1170 and left behind, with the Indians, the Welsh language.'

Back in Wales, in Rhos-on-Sea, there are the remains of the old stone quay, discovered in exactly the place that is was said that Madoc had sailed. Today, the quay is in the garden of 'Odstone', a bungalow at Rhos, as the creek has long since silted up and is now part of a golf course. The wall bears another plaque, which reads:

'*Prince Madoc sailed from here Aber Kerrick Gwynan
1170 AD and landed at Mobile, Alabama with his ships
Gorn Gwynant and Pedr Sant.*'

MORE EVIDENCE?

George Catlin, a nineteenth-century lawyer, reportedly
spent eight years living among various Native American
tribes including the Mandans. When he returned to
Britain, he declared that he had uncovered the descendants
of Prince Madog's expedition. Unfortunately the tribe was
virtually wiped out by a smallpox epidemic introduced by
traders in 1837.

Another startling discovery came in 1889, when a stone
was excavated from an undisturbed burial mound in Bat
Creek, Eastern Tennessee. The director of the project at the
time declared that the inscription on the stone was 'beyond
question letters of the Cherokee alphabet'. It wasn't until
the 1960s that new research found that it definitely wasn't
Cherokee, but something else.

Hebrew scholars considered the possibility that the Bat
Creek stone, as it came to be known, was inscribed with
Paleo-Hebrew; however, the meaning couldn't be deduced.
Carbon-14 dating had already placed the inscription on
the stone at the right period for Madoc, by dating pieces of
wood found around the stone.

Then, in 2002, researchers Alan Wilson, Baram A. Blackett
and Jim Michael announced that the Bat Creek stone
was in fact inscribed with the ancient Welsh *Coelbren*
alphabet, and reads, in Welsh, '*Madoc the Ruler he is*'.
The researchers then went on to declare that the Bat Creek
mound was 'the likely tomb of Prince Madoc'.

Wilson also said: 'The components of the alphabet derive from the earliest days of the Khumric (Welsh) people ... and were used along their migration routes to Wales in antiquity.'

ICELAND GETS INVOLVED IN THE DEBATE!

The Icelandic Orkneyinga Sagas from 1139-1148 records frequent attacks by a 'Freeman of Wales' on their settlements in the 'southern isles' including Tyree and the Isle of Man. In retaliation, they attacked Wales and the freeman ran for refuge to Lundy, which he used as a base. This seems a little too early for Madoc, but it proves that Welsh sailors were making frequent voyages around the Irish Sea area at that time – and Lundy crops up once again.

Cynric ap Gronow, the mid-fifteenth-century poet, is said to have written a poem that included the line: 'Horn Gwennan, brought to the Gele, To be given a square mast, Was turned back to Afon Ganol's quay For Madog's famous voyage.'

However, we only have this as a 1674 translation by Evan Williams and it cannot be definitely proven to date from before Columbus' voyage.

THE 'OTHER' STORIES

There are other stories, which are almost certainly apocryphal, but make good reading. In 1686, a Revd Morgan Jones wrote some memoirs to a friend, explaining that two decades earlier he had been captured by a tribe with fair features. He feared for his life, and prayed out loud in Welsh that he might be released. To his great surprise, his captors started speaking Welsh and they treated him like a king.

For every story of good fortune, however, there seems to be one of sadness. A young Methodist minister, John Evans, was sponsored to travel to the Welsh Indians. In poor health, after charting thousands of miles of the new land, he finally declared 'there is no such thing as the Welsh Indians!'

THE WELSH IN AMERICA: DID YOU KNOW?

Senator John Sharp Williams of Mississippi (1854-1932) was a prominent American politician in the Democratic Party from the 1890s to the 1920s. He had been orphaned during the American Civil War.

He was well travelled and had studied at five different universities, including two in Europe. He is recorded as saying in Senate (and it was duly recorded in the daily Congressional Record) that in proportion to its population numbers Wales had contributed more to the development of the United States than any other nation.

Sharp was convinced that the Welsh had played a significant part in building the modern United States of America.

WELL, DID YOU KNOW THIS?

The Welsh Society of Philadelphia is the oldest ethnic society in the United States. In 1729 a group of Welsh people living in the city founded the Society of Ancient Britons to honour St David, patron saint of Wales. On 1 March, St David's Day, Welsh people met at the Queen's Head Tavern in King Street, Philadelphia, followed by a service in Christchurch, at which the sermon was preached in Welsh.

The society was so influential that the President, Benjamin Franklin, often attended their banquets. After the Revolution, in which many Welshman fought for independence, the group reorganised and sixty-four members drew up a constitution on 4 February 1799.

The constitution stated that newly arrived Welsh immigrants should be supported; 'instructing him in what he is ignorant of and providing for his immediate necessities.'

As part of its remit, members of the society were expected to provide financial assistance, moral support and practical relief for the Welsh immigrants, who were usually struggling. After all, many had left Wales to avoid the harsh economic conditions, so they usually turned up in America with very little or nothing.

The society, now called the Welsh Society *(Cymdeithas Gymraeg)* Philadelphia has had a long history, promoting Welsh cultural links and arranging its annual St David's Day celebrations.

It is good to know that the society is still the spiritual home of the Welsh in America, after many years being a practical and supportive aid for many who found themselves strangers in a strange land.

MORE WELSH-AMERICAN CONNECTIONS

The American War of Independence (1755-1783) had at its heart a deep division between the colonists in America and the British Government. The colonists saw their purpose as carving out a brave new world in a sometimes inhospitable land. However, the government saw the role of the colony to provide raw materials to Britain and British manufacturers.

In a sense, there were no Americans then, only the different ethnic groups who would form a new nation when the American Declaration of Independence was signed.

The largest ethnic group of signatories (sixteen in all) on the original draft of the American Declaration of Independence were Welsh.

Thomas Jefferson himself, who helped draft the document, and went on to become the third President of the US, was in fact a Welsh speaker, his family being from Snowdonia.

Without a doubt, the Welsh have had a hand in America from the beginning of the nation, and ever since. The following are some of the people of Welsh descent that have figured in the politics of America since the Declaration of Independence.

John Adams – served terms as President of the United States and Vice-President of the United States between 1735 and 1826.

John Quincy Adams – served as President of the United States and Secretary of State between 1767 and 1848.

Cassius Marcellus Clay – the prominent anti-slavery activist was born in 1810 of Welsh ancestry.

Hillary Rodham Clinton (born in 1947) – Secretary of State, US Senator from New York, former First Lady, candidate for the 2008 Democratic presidential nomination. Both her father and mother are of Welsh descent.

Calvin Coolidge – twenty-ninth Vice-President of the United States and thirtieth President of the United States (1923-1929) was of Welsh descent.

James J. Davis – American Secretary of Labor and Senator was born in Tredegar in 1873.

Jefferson Davis – soldier, politician, and first and only President of the Confederate States (1862-1865).

William Floyd – United States Declaration of Independence signatory. His family were from Brecon.

Button Gwinnett – United States Declaration of Independence signatory, born to Welsh parents in 1735.

Charles Evans Hughes – Governor of New York, born to Welsh parents in 1862.

Thomas Jefferson – third President of the United States, first Secretary of State. Born in 1743, his ancestors possibly came from Snowdonia.

Francis Lewis – United States Declaration of Independence signatory, born in Llandaff in Cardiff in 1713.

Abraham Lincoln – sixteenth President of the United States. The most famous of the Welsh Americans imported an inscribed stone to be added to the Washington Memorial. It reads: *Fy iaith, fy ngwlad, fy nghenedl Cymru – Cymru am byth* (My language, my land, my nation of Wales – Wales forever).

Barack Obama – forty-fourth President of the United States (Welsh ancestry on mother's side). Born in 1961, the first black president of the USA.

Thomas Wynne – Physician to William Penn and speaker of the first Pennsylvania Provincial Assembly. Born in Ysceifiog, where his family were descended from Owain Gwynedd.

There are also several others that one may be less inclined to laud as having Welsh ancestry, namely:

Benedict Arnold – Revolution general who surrendered West Point to the Crown during the War of Independence.

E. Howard Hunt – CIA Intelligence Officer. A key figure in organising and participating in the Watergate burglaries.

Having helped to set up the new country politically, the Welsh then went on to figure prominently in the arts, in particular pioneering the two original art forms that America gave the world, jazz music and Hollywood movies.

Jazz pianist and composer Bill Evans and Quincy Jones, the conductor, arranger, film composer, television producer, and jazz trumpeter, both had a Welsh parent.

The list of Welsh actors and actresses that became Hollywood movie stars is long and well documented, however 'not a lot of people know that' (to quote a prominent English film star) a lot of the early pioneers of the movies had Welsh ancestry:

'D.W.' Griffith, regarded as the premier pioneering American film director following his epic 1915 film *The Birth of a Nation* and his subsequent film *Intolerance*, was born David Llewelyn Wark Griffith to Anglo-Welsh parents.

Glenn Ford, star of many classic Hollywood films. His mother was born in Pontypridd.

Harold Lloyd, one of the most popular and influential film comedians of the silent film era, had Welsh paternal grandparents.

Bob Hope, the famous American comedian, was born in Eltham, London, but his mother was a light opera singer from Barry, South Wales.

The Welsh also left their mark on the American 'Wild West': both Jesse James the outlaw and Daniel Boone the famous pioneer were of Welsh descent.

Coming back up to date, there is an on-going Welsh connection with Wall Street, the financial centre in Manhattan, New York. Descendants of the west Wales adventurer Robert Edwards are going to court to prove their ownership of Wall Street.

According to the website www.famouswelsh.com, the Edwards family's claim is that when the property – pasture land at the time – was leased to the Kruger brothers, the terms stated the lease would expire in 100 years. The brothers in turn allowed the Roman Catholic Church to use the land as it saw fit. The Church has controlled the land since, building on it themselves and renting to other parties too; this is the Manhattan we know today. The rent for this use is stored in a vault in Manhattan itself, now estimated at over $800 billion!

Robert Edwards died childless, leaving his property to his sister in Wales and her descendents, who are estimated now to number some 3,000. If they win, it means a pay-out of over $26 million each!

A DIFFERENT TYPE OF
CAREER IN FINANCE?

Al Capone, the gangster who led a Prohibition-era crime syndicate in 1920s Chicago, was supported by his chief lieutenant, known as 'Murray the Hump'. Llewelyn Morris 'Murray' Humphreys was one of the most successful criminals in US history. He was born in Chicago of Welsh parents from Llandinam, Powys, mid-Wales.

Al Capone said Murray would rather negotiate than kill people: 'Anybody can use a gun. "The Hump" can shoot if he has to, but he likes to negotiate with cash when he can.'

Humphreys believed in the corruptibility of figures of authority, his favourite maxim being: 'The difference between guilt and innocence in any court is who gets to the judge first with the most.'

Where some of his peers lived like film stars, Humphreys chose to spend most of his life in a nondescript bungalow in South Shore, Chicago.

When Humphreys died of a heart attack in 1965 at the age of sixty-six, Sandy Smith, the *Chicago Tribune*'s top crime journalist, reported Humphreys' death in an article entitled, *'His Epitaph: No Gangster Was More Bold.'* Another newspaperman, Mike Royko, had the following quip to offer: '[Humphreys] died of unnatural causes – a heart attack.'

Some facts about Murray the Hump, Welsh gangster:

His daughter Llewella spoke highly of her father in 1999, praising his sensitivity, generosity and charm.

Chicago tradition has it that the political phrase 'vote early, vote often' originated with him.

He was described as 'the nicest guy in the mob'.

He once said, 'If you ever have to cock a gun in a man's face, kill him. If you walk away without killing him after doing that, he'll kill you the next day.'

Throughout his career, Humphreys was only imprisoned once, for a minor tax-evasion charge in the 1930s.

So that's some of the story of the travelling Welsh leaving the green green grass of home; they travelled far and wide. Emigration to the Americas and elsewhere was a chance for people to escape the harsh economic conditions. From the north and south, the Welsh left to find a better future for themselves and their families.

And back in Wales...

7

FOOD, RUGBY AND COAL
BWYD, BENDIGEDIG BWYD – FOOD, GLORIOUS FOOD

There is no doubt that the Welsh love their food! They pride themselves in the freshness, quality and variety of their produce. The climate and landscape of Wales reflects this, from fish and seafood brought to shore on the rugged coast, the vegetables and fruit that are harvested from the green land, and the animals which are farmed on the levels, valleys, hills and mountains. Wales is an extraordinary place to grow food, fish or rear animals.

It's not a recent thing, either; food in Wales has quite a history. In the tenth century, the laws of Hywel Dda mention the vegetables that were to be cultivated in Wales, so that the land could be used to best effect. The mountains and hills were harsh places where it was difficult to grow crops apart from oats and other cereals, so Welsh cuisine was never 'fussy food', but good, nutritious and cheap meals that could feed hardworking men and women, helping them survive the harsh realities of rural life in Wales.

So, what about classic Welsh recipes? A search in a good bookshop or on the internet will reveal dozens of ways to prepare the food that has sustained the Welsh for many generations. Here are some you might find:

CAWL AND LOBSGOWS

Cawl is a sort of stew and soup all at the same time; it has many variants, but usually includes bacon, lamb or beef, cabbage, swede and that essential Welsh ingredient, the leek. Slow cooking is the trick here, and slow eating too! The cawl usually improves with age, and eating it on the second or even the third day tastes so much better than the first. The vegetables and meat are usually very chunky and the stock is thickened.

Lobsgows is the North Wales equivalent of cawl, and is very similar apart from the meat and vegetables being cut into smaller chunks, and the stock is not thickened. It was traditionally eaten during the winter to sustain people in the difficult conditions.

We know for certain that the Welsh have been eating cawl for at least 700 years; there is documentary evidence for that. Today, cawl is more likely to contain lamb and leeks, and not the mixture of ingredients that were found in this super-stew in years past.

WELSH RAREBIT

This has to be one of the most famous Welsh dishes. However, it isn't what people think it is! It is more than merely cheese on toast.

With strong cheese, melted with butter, pepper, mustard and beer (or even white wine or welsh whisky), this luxurious and filling snack is quite an enigma.

Chefs, cooks and kitchen amateurs from all places seem to have a particular twist on this dish. Even Mrs Beeton suggested that port should be added. However, I'm sure this would make a rather interesting pink looking rarebit. There seems to be no fixed recipe or agreed standard, other than after simmering whatever you've decided upon, this fantastic Welsh fondue is then poured over good-quality home-made bread and served before it cools.

There are, of course, several variations: the Buck Rarebit is Welsh Rarebit with a poached egg on top, and one early cookbook even mentions pouring the rarebit over apple or mincemeat pies.

BARA BRITH

This fruit loaf, whose name literally means mottled or speckled bread, is a mainstay of Welsh teashops and cafés. Church cake-stalls look somehow empty without it, and almost every Welsh family has a recipe for it.

Traditionally, in Wales the ovens were lit once a week to bake enough bread for the family, and at the end of the day, as the oven cooled down, the remaining bread dough would be baked with spices, currants and sometimes honey. Served in buttered slices to this day, Bara Brith can't be missed on a trip to Wales.

Recipes today tend to suggest the use of cold tea, marmalade and eggs to make the loaf richer, and there are even recipes that suggest sugar-encrusting and honey glazing too.

GLAMORGAN SAUSAGES

This vegetarian delight is a great find for those who want good tasty meat-free food that reflects the quality of the ingredients. The Victorian gentleman-writer George Borrow mentioned Glamorgan sausages in his book *Wild Wales,* published in 1862; he wrote, 'The breakfast was delicious, consisting of excellent tea, buttered toast and Glamorgan sausages, which I really think are not a whit inferior to those of Epping.'

Probably made originally with Caerphilly cheese, these sausages also contain leeks, breadcrumbs, herbs (usually parsley, thyme and sage), mustard and eggs. Served with salad, vegetables, rice or even on their own, they are well worth a try.

WAGON WHEELS AND
THE POT NOODLE MINES

We should also remember that Wales is also famous for other foods produced there from time to time.

Wagon Wheels – If there's a bigger bite, it can't be found!

These circles of chocolate goodness have been produced near Cwmbran since 1948, originally as Weston's Wagon Wheels. There are other factories that satisfy the international demand, with Australia, Canada and Iran all having factories producing Wagon Wheels.

The large marshmallow biscuits, covered with a chocolate-flavoured coating, were immortalised in comedy when Jennifer Saunders stuffed a whole Wagon Wheel into her mouth in the comedy sketch show *French and Saunders*. This was no mean feat, because they are 74mm (nearly 3in) in diameter.

Wagon Wheels were re-launched successfully in 2002, after fifty-four years in the lunchboxes and larger biscuit jars of the nation.

Pot Noodle – a Welsh export
It's difficult to know where to begin in describing this prince of snack foods. These robust plastic cups of dehydrated noodles and vegetables, flavouring and a sauce sachet are almost legendary.

Launched in 1978, Pot Noodles are now produced in Croespenmaen near Crumlin, South Wales where around 150 million pots are produced annually. The Welsh connection was successfully exploited in 2006, when an advertising campaign showed Welsh people working in the fictitious Pot Noodle mines. Even though a complaint was made to the Advertising Standards Authority (ASA), suggesting the adverts were racist, the complaint was rejected.

Other advertising campaigns have been less well received. In 2002, the 'Slag of all Snacks' campaign was criticised and subsequently withdrawn. As was the rather curious 'Hurt me, you slag' campaign which left the ASA believing it might drive people to violence.

True to form, the 2005 campaign was also considered by many to be offensive, but this time the ASA came down on the side of the Welsh noodle masters, judging that 'Have you got the Pot Noodle Horn?' was only 'a little crude'.

Despite the 2004 poll that described Pot Noodle as the *most hated brand*, it seems that sales have been completely immune from criticism.

In comedy and popular culture Pot Noodle has been derided as food for the poor and lazy. In the series *Red Dwarf* the character Lister describes Pot Noodle thus: 'I tell you one thing: I've been to a parallel universe, I've seen time running backwards, I've played pool with planets, and I've given birth to twins, but I never thought in my entire life I'd taste an edible Pot Noodle.'

On the other hand, Pot Noodle has had some good comments too. Noel Gallagher from the popular Britpop band Oasis, when asked if he 'loved his brother Liam', replied, 'Sure I love Liam, but not as much as I love Pot Noodle.'

Similarly, the character Del Boy in the British sitcom *Only Fools and Horses* describes the hectic life of the modern entrepreneur when he says, 'Yeah, I eat on the move. Mobile phone in one hand and Pot Noodle in the other.'

With over a dozen flavours and variations, this Welsh export has become somewhat of an enigma.

FOODIE DID YOU KNOWS

Did you know? One of the strangest laws on the statute books makes it illegal to eat a mince pie in England on Christmas Day; however, it is perfectly legal to do so in Wales.

Did you know? Laver Bread, the Welsh delicacy, is a type of seaweed. It needs to be boiled for several hours, and then generally it is served with cockles or bacon. Sometimes it is rolled with oats to produce small cakes that can be fried. A great source of iron and protein, it can be found in many shops.

Did you know? When sixty-eight-year-old Ian Neale from Cardiff broke the world record for growing the largest swede, he received a personal video message from American rapper Snoop Dogg offering Mr Neale two free tickets to his Cardiff show if he would share the 'secrets of growing vegetation so big … so that I can grow my vegetation big too.'

Did you know? Many fruits and vegetables we enjoy today were introduced into Wales by the Romans. Cabbages, cucumbers, leeks, plums, cherries and the grape are all examples of this.

THE FOOD REVOLUTION!

For many years, Welsh cuisine was thought to be of little importance, with very little to offer in terms of excitement or excellence. So what had left Welsh cooking in the wilderness for such a long time?

The difficulty was that most English culinary traditions developed from the upper echelons of its society and reflected a plentiful and varied supply of food. The true tastes of Wales, however, derived from the harsh landscape. Welsh food was intended to satisfy the needs of hardworking men and women. Hearty and filling dishes were necessary to appease the appetites of farm labourers, coal miners, iron and steel workers and fishermen. Wales' bleak uplands ensured that, apart from oats, very few cereal crops could flourish. Consequently, oats became part of the staple diet when incorporated with soups, porridge and cakes. For years, Welsh food was thought to be uninspiring, and the mere phrase 'Welsh cuisine' was thought to be an oxymoron.

Slowly but surely the story of food in Wales started a new chapter...

In recent years the clever Welsh have created something of a resurgence in food and drink production. Welsh cheese and beer have been joined by Welsh curry, chocolate, organic yogurts, pate, mustard, and even Welsh biltong (traditionally a South African snack made from beef).

These fantastic foodstuffs have added to the tradition of good home cooking from quality ingredients like lamb, leek, cockles, laverbread, monkfish and potatoes.

It isn't just the home cooking and the factories producing unique foods. Wales has become something of a gastro-tourism destination, listed as one of the top three in the world. With the well-respected and well-attended Abergavenny Food Festival firing up the movement, attention was drawn to the wealth of good restaurants and renowned chefs who have made their home in Wales. Since then, good food has been big business.

In an interview with the *Guardian* newspaper in August 2012, Shaun Hill, from the Michelin-starred The Walnut Tree restaurant near Abergavenny, said:

> People are discovering how good their produce is. We have first-class lamb, good beef, game, cheese and some very good charcuterie. Wales has always been a poor country so the culture is simple food – baking, and good meat or fish. … Ah, the produce, testament to Wales's grassy slopes [and] mountainous farmland…

According to the Welsh Government's tourism website www.visitwales.co.uk, these are the top ten award-winning Welsh restaurants:

The Walnut Tree Inn
Llandewi Skirrid, Abergavenny, Monmouthshire

The Crown at Whitebrook
Whitebrook, Monmouthshire

Chai Street / Mint & Mustard
Cardiff

The Foxhunter
Nantderry, Monmouthshire

The Bell at Skenfrith
Skenfrith, Monmouthshire

Y Polyn
Capel Dewi, Carmarthenshire

Fairyhill
Reynoldston, Gower Cottage, Swansea

Ynyshir Hall
Eglwysfach, Machynlleth, Powys

Tyddyn Llan
Llandrillo, Corwen

SPORTING WALES

There are many sports played in Wales – indeed, the Welsh are generally very good at most sports. With Wikipedia alone listing over 300 Welsh sporting heroes, it's difficult to know where to start! Well, how about starting a few hundred years ago?

GUTO NYTH BRÂN (1700-1737)

Griffith Morgan was known as Guto Nyth Brân after his parents' farm in the Rhondda Valley, The Crow's Nest. His feats have become legendary, and have gone down in Welsh history.

His nimbleness as an athlete was developed as a youngster when he herded sheep with his father; stories soon appeared of him catching hares, foxes and birds, such was his speed and agility.

Guto once ran from his home to Pontypridd and back, a distance of around 7 miles, before a kettle boiled. He continued entering races and accepting challenges, but before too long it became apparent that no one could beat him in races of any length or terrain.

Love was in the air when the local shopkeeper Siân o'r Siop (Sian of the Shop) arranged a race for Guto. By the age of thirty, Guto went into retirement with Siân, but eventually came out of retirement in 1737, at the age of thirty-seven, to race for a prize of over £1,000. These riches would secure a comfortable retirement for Siân and Guto, and even though they both had reservations about this, he went into training again.

Guto's challenger, the Prince of Bedwas, was a formidable opponent, and pushed Guto from the start. Eventually, however, Guto's class and speed shone through and he won the race. He was mobbed at the end of the race, and in the crush he was tragically killed, dying in the arms of his beloved Siân.

He was buried in Llanwynno church, near Mountain Ash, in the Cynon Valley.

Each year, the *Nos Galan* (New Year's Eve) races take place to commemorate the life of this legendary athlete. Races around a 3-mile (5km) course around the town are extremely popular, and each year the runners are joined by a famous mystery sporting celebrity, whose identity is kept secret until the last moment before the start of the race. Welsh rugby stars such as Shane Williams (2011) and James Hook (2009) have been joined by athletes Christian Malcolm (2000), Darren Campbell (2001), Jamie Baulch (1998) and Iwan Thomas (1997). The famous Olympian road bicycle racer Nicole Cooke ran in 2004. The mystery runner then lays the wreath to Guto Nyth Brân at the end of the race.

Guto Nyth Brân, the greatest of all Welsh sporting heroes, occupies a position somewhere between historical fact and legend. His extraordinary life serves as an encouragement to young athletes to this day. A statue of Guto was commissioned, sculpted by Peter Nicholas, and placed in Mountain Ash town centre in 1990 to remind people of his life and feats.

THE WELSH AT THE OLYMPICS

In the 2012 London Olympics, the Welsh athletes managed a record medals haul for such a small nation:

Geraint Thomas, cycling, gold
Freddie Evans, boxing, silver
Tom James, rowing (coxless fours), gold
Jade Jones, taekwondo, gold
Chris Bartley, rowing (lightweight men's four), silver
Hannah Mills sailing (470 class), silver
Sarah Thomas, hockey, bronze

To put this in perspective, with seven medals Wales is in roughly the same place as India, Mexico, Sweden, Croatia and the Democratic Peoples Republic of Korea.

In the Paralympics, the Welsh members of Team GB did well also. Led by Mark Colbourne (Gold, Cycling), Aled Sion Davies (Gold, Athletics) and Josie Pearson (Gold, Athletics) they won a total of fourteen medals, putting us next to Greece, Nigeria, Austria, Switzerland and Sweden in the medals table.

RUGBY AND THE ODD-SHAPED BALL

There can be no doubt that the national sport of Wales is rugby, and it would be wrong not to include some information about the game, the people, the places and the fascination with which it grips the Welsh nation.

Rugby is a physically demanding, fast-moving game. Two teams of fifteen slug it out to score tries and kick conversions. Penalties are awarded for untoward behaviour, and when a Welsh international match is being played in the Millennium Stadium in Cardiff, and 70,000 Welsh voices are singing 'Bread of Heaven', or the National Anthem *Hen Wlad Fy Nhadau*, the whole of the capital city seems to resonate to the sound. When Wales have possession of the ball the crowd sing, cheer and shout, and in the moments before a conversion or penalty kick are made, you could hear a pin drop.

This is poetically summed up in the words of Welsh actor Richard Burton: 'Rugby is a wonderful show: dance, opera and, suddenly, the blood of a killing.'

A RUGBY HALL OF FAME

The term *cap* refers to a player's appearance in a national team. Some Welsh rugby players have a long and illustrious history in the national sport; their names have gone down in history.

Here are ten Welsh rugby players who have received the most caps, and the years they played:

1	Stephen Jones	(1998-2011)	104 caps
2=	Gareth Thomas	(1995-2007)	100 caps
2=	Martyn Williams	(1996–2012)	100 caps
4	Colin Charvis	(1996-2007)	94 caps
5	Gareth Llewellyn	(1989-2004)	92 caps
6	Gethin Jenkins	(2002-2012)	91 caps
7=	Neil Jenkins	(1991-2002)	87 caps
7=	Shane Williams	(2000-2011)	87 caps
9	Adam Jones	(2003-2012)	83 caps
10	Dwayne Peel	(2001-2011)	76 caps

IRON AND COAL

Iron and coal changed Wales: visit any former mining area and you will see how the landscape has been transformed. Imagine yourselves there at the height of coal and iron production; imagine yourselves witnessing the flashing in the sky of the furnaces as the doors were opened, and imagine the dark spoil heaps marking the horizon.

Close-knit communities with shared values and concerns mark out the Welsh valleys as different. Friendliness and determination, courage and pride, are all in abundance. These characteristics have been roughly hewn from hundreds of years of not merely surviving, but flourishing, as a people. Facing the challenges together.

VISIT BIG PIT

Big Pit (*Pwll Mawr*) is an industrial heritage museum in Blaenavon (*Blaenafon*), South Wales. It is run by the National Museum of Wales, and was a working coalmine from 1860 to 1980. It is dedicated to the preservation of this great Welsh heritage and visitors will find it very close to the conditions that miners would have found when the pit was operational.

Upon entry to the museum, visitors are expected to surrender all contraband, watches, mobile phones and lighters. Posters inform people of the dangers of carbon monoxide poisoning, and automatic gas monitoring systems are discretely placed around the tunnels, as are emergency telephones.

The museum is well designed and preserved as an operational attraction. The pit props are real and the steel bands are not for show: they hold up the mine roof. This is a place where miners worked for over 120 years, men died in explosions and fires when coal was being extracted, and the landscape over the town shows the scars of iron and coal workings.

Blaenavon (*Blaenafon*) is an astonishing town, and is a UNESCO World Heritage Site.

8

LAND OF WRITERS AND POETS

It's in the genes for the Welsh! If they aren't singing, they are writing. If they aren't writing stories, they are writing poetry! Here are some notable Welsh wordsmiths:

Dannie Abse (b.1923) – poet, writer and doctor
Dannie Abse was born into a Jewish family in Cardiff. A well-known poet, he also worked for many years as a specialist doctor in a chest clinic. His first collection of poetry, *After Every Green Thing,* was published in 1949, and since then he has published a significant body of work, collecting many awards and accolades. Abse was appointed CBE in the 2012 New Year's Honours list for his services to poetry and literature.

'Most Welshmen are worthless,
an inferior breed, doctor.
He did not know I was Welsh.
Then he praised the architects
of the German death-camps
— did not know I was a Jew.'

Dannie Abse

Alexander Cordell (1914-1997) – novelist and author of
thirty acclaimed works including Rape of the Fair Country,
The Hosts of Rebecca *and* Song of the Earth
With twenty-eight novels under his belt, Cordell was
one of Wales' most prolific authors. His well-researched
historic novels about Wales are full of the socio-economic
realities of the time. They are exciting, well-structured and
poignant, following families and the grim realities and
challenges they faced.

His best-known novel, *Rape of the Fair Country*, is the first
book in a trilogy following the Mortimer family through
the struggles for justice in the iron works, to the Chartist
rising in Newport, then the Rebecca Riots, a major series of
protests in West Wales against unfair agricultural taxation.

'His words were level and smooth, like most English. There
is a horrid way of speaking – every word deep and pure, but
without music.'

Alexander Cordell

Roald Dahl (1916-1990) – author. Born in Cardiff to
Norwegian parents, his notable works include Charlie
and the Chocolate Factory, James and the Giant Peach,
Fantastic Mr Fox, Matilda *and* The Witches
The life of Dahl is almost as fantastic as one of his books.
He attended Llandaff Cathedral School in Cardiff, where he
famously placed a dead mouse in a jar of sweets in a shop
where the rather unpleasant shopkeeper had upset him.
The school boys immortalised the event by describing it as
The Great Mouse Plot of 1924.

Dahl, at this point, showed no sign that he would become a
famous and well-loved writer of poems and stories. He did
however achieve notoriety in another way. Rising through
the ranks of the Royal Air Force in the Second World War,
he achieved fame when he became a flying ace and an

Intelligence Officer. Settling down to writing after the war, he began to write the wonderful stories he is remembered for.

> 'The Bristol Channel was always my guide, and I was always able to draw an imaginary line from my bed to our house over in Wales. It was a great comfort.'
>
> Roald Dahl

W.H. Davies (1871-1940) – poet and tramp

It's hard to know where to begin when you try to describe the life of W.H. Davies in a few short words. Beginning life in the then busy port of Newport, Monmouthshire, tragedy struck early when his father died. His grandparents, who ran a pub, brought up the three-year-old William and his two siblings.

William's grandfather had been a sea-captain, and he would have heard tales of far-off lands and the peoples. In and out of trouble with the authorities, the young William was once given twelve strokes of the lash for stealing with his gang. At fifteen he became an apprentice to a picture framer, but he was restless and left shortly after. Several other jobs followed until he realised that he had a wanderlust that must be satisfied.

Setting his sights far afield, he sailed from Bristol to America, working on ships transporting cattle. Leaving the seafaring life he became Wales' Supertramp poet. As a tramp, or hobo or bum, as the Americans probably called him, he was one of the thousands of homeless who wandered North America, looking for shelter, food and work. Eventually, William made his way to the Klondike to search for gold, but disaster wasn't far away.

Attempting to jump a train one day, he fell under the wheels and lost the lower half of one leg. He returned to Wales and tried to sell his poetry, but only enjoyed modest success.

Living now in London as a tramp, it wasn't until 1907, when George Bernard Shaw wrote a preface to his book *Autobiography of a Supertramp*, that his career took off! The years of begging and scratching around for work had finished, but he didn't seek the highlife, continuing to live in and around London in very shabby properties. His work stretched to over 700 pieces.

He is best known for two lines in his poem *Leisure*:

'What is this life if, full of care,
We have no time to stand and stare?

W.H. Davies

Gerald of Wales (c. 1146-c. 1223) – chronicler, bishop and writer

Jumping backwards a few hundred years, we have the man known as *Gerald of Wales, Giraldus Cambrensis, Gerallt Gymro* and a few other names too! This is probably because he had tried his hand at everything possible. A theologian and priest, he was also a diplomat, reformer, travel writer, chronicler and even an outlaw! Although Gerald was Welsh by birth, people still question whether he was an agent of the English throne, or if he indeed was a loyal Welshman. Whichever of these is true, it seems that he was rather single-minded and ready to accept almost any challenge.

In his books on Wales, *Itinerarium Kamnriae* and *Descripto Kambriae* (1193), he writes in Latin about Wales and the Welsh. Gerald recorded everything in great detail, and his work gives a clear picture of life in medieval Wales:

This seems to me a thing to be noticed, that just as the men of this country are, during this mortal life, more prone to anger and revenge than any other race, so in eternal death the saints of this land, that have been elevated by their merits, are more vindictive than the saints of any other region.

He goes on to write about what might have been an early male voice choir: 'In their musical concerts they do not sing in unison like the inhabitants of other countries, but in many different parts.'

Gerald also notes that: 'In Wales no one begs' and the homes of the Welsh are 'open to everyone'. He also writes: 'For the Welsh, generosity and hospitality are the greatest of all virtues.'

Arthur Machen, (1863-1947) – horror/fantasy writer and literary critic, journalist and actor
Arthur Machen was born in Caerleon, the grandson of the vicar of Caerleon, and the son of the rector of Llandewi Fach, a village close by. His grandfather and father were antiquarians, involved with the excavations of the Roman ruins there. Machen would have seen the artefacts of a long-gone age being brought to the surface and placed in the Roman Legionary Museum there.

Machen attended Hereford Cathedral School. However, his family were unable to afford the fees to send him to university, so he made his way to London to find a career. Failing medical school exams, he worked as a journalist and clerk in a publishing house. His fascination with the fantastic and macabre continued, and he started to write poems and short stories.

Over the years, Machen amassed quite a body of work, including several notable tales. In 1914, Machen wrote a story about the appearance of the ghosts of the archers of Agincourt during a First World War battle. Soon after, people claimed to have seen the ghostly figures who assisted the British in the battle. The more Machen declared his work was fiction, the more people came forward stating that they had seen them.

Machen's best remembered work, however, is his novella, published in the magazine *Whirlwind* in 1890. It was instantly declared to be 'degenerate and horrible'. The story tells of a Welsh woman who is subjected to an experiment by a scientist to enable her to see the God of Nature, Pan. Years later her daughter travels to London and wreaks havoc there, the monstrous incarnation of Pan.

> 'Of Mr Machen's horror-tales the most famous is perhaps 'The Great God Pan' which tells of a singular and terrible experiment and its consequences.'
>
> H.P. Lovecraft

More recently, the horror writer Stephen King wrote that *The Great God Pan* is; '... one of the best horror stories ever written. Maybe the best in the English language.'

Machen inspired many others, who have shared an interest in his work. His unique blend of high-church Anglicanism, mysticism and fantasy, combined with his interest in Celtic myth and legend, the Holy Grail, and the lives of the Welsh saints, makes his work unique. It is a shame that Machen isn't more widely read; without a doubt, this son of Wales is one of its best-kept literary secrets.

On his work, Machen wrote: 'I dream in fire, but work in clay.'

On mystery and fantasy: 'Every branch of human knowledge, if traced up to its source and final principles, vanishes into mystery.'

Writing about the Stock Exchange (!):

> But he recognised that the illusions of the child only differed from those of the man in that they were more picturesque; belief in fairies and belief in the Stock Exchange as bestowers of happiness were equally vain, but the latter form of faith was ugly as well as inept.
>
> *Hill of Dreams*

Dylan Thomas (1914-1953) – poet, writer
Probably Wales' most famous literary son, Thomas wrote some of the most enduring poetry of the twentieth century. His poem 'Do Not Go Gentle into that Good Night', written for his dying father, encourages him to fight right to the end of his life, with the words 'Rage, Rage, against the dying of the light'. Its popularity comes from its accessibility, but also the intensity with which it is written, an intensity that almost makes it jump off the page.

His plays continue to attract much critical acclaim; *Under Milk Wood* and *A Child's Christmas in Wales* are considered to be his finest works. In *Under Milk Wood* the narrator invites the audience to hear the dreams and private thoughts of the residents of a fictional Welsh fishing village called Llareggub. (The name is 'bugger all' spelt backwards!)

The beautifully nostalgic *A Child's Christmas in Wales* presents a wonderful sketch of the festive season. The Welsh Christmas is like a changeless fairy tale; it is always snowing, and the people of the small town gather together to celebrate:

> One Christmas was so much like another, in those years around the sea-town corner now and out of all sound except the distant speaking of the voices I sometimes hear a moment before sleep, that I can never remember whether it snowed for six days and six nights when I was twelve or whether it snowed for twelve days and twelve nights when I was six.
>
> *A Child's Christmas in Wales*

Thomas gained popularity and his works were well loved. However, earning enough to survive from royalties proved very difficult. In the latter half of the 1940s he found work recording readings and broadcasts at the BBC in London; this brought him a significant income, and with it a celebrity status.

In the early 1950s trips to America brought about lasting fame when he recorded *A Child's Christmas in Wales*, and he undertook several tours. Bearing the pressures and weight of fame took their toll on Thomas, who died prematurely in 1953 in New York.

It is well worth visiting Wales to see the Dylan Thomas Theatre and Dylan Thomas Centre in Swansea, where the annual Dylan Thomas Festival is held. There is a memorial in Cwmdonkin Park, Swansea, close to the birthplace of Thomas. There is also the Laugharne Boathouse, and his writing shed, in Laugharne, Camarthenshire, where Thomas lived from 1949 until 1953. The town and the people are thought to have been the inspiration for his work during that time:

> You can tear a poem apart to see what makes it technically tick... You're back with the mystery of having been moved by words. The best craftsmanship always leaves holes and gaps in the works of the poem so that something that is not in the poem can creep, crawl, flash, or thunder in. The joy and function of poetry is, and was, the celebration of man, which is also the celebration of God.
>
> *Poetic Manifesto*

9

THE DROVERS
IN WALES

HEIPTRO HO –
THE DROVERS ARE COMING

Scenes of cowboys driving herds of cattle along the Shawnee Trail and the Chisholm Trail to market in the Midwest of America have been made famous by numerous Hollywood movies. But did you know that Welshmen had been driving livestock over remote tracks from north, mid and the west of Wales to sell in the English market towns for hundreds of years before the advent of the American cowboy? In fact, the drovers only stopped with the advent of the railways in the Victorian era.

The trackways used by the drovers, which over the years became well worn by the hooves of thousands of animals, were known as drovers 'roads' (despite the fact that hardly any were originally suitable for even horse-drawn carts).

The drovers marked their approach into villages and towns with a shout of '*Heiptro Ho!*' This warning gave people time to move any of their own livestock and children safely out of the way. The coming of the drovers was an impressive sight and an exciting event for the younger children in the communities they passed through.

Picture a procession of hundreds of animals that could easily stretch a half a mile from front to back, comprising cattle, sheep, pigs and even geese. The animals, all moving at a walking pace, were herded by men on sturdy Welsh ponies, whilst other men walked alongside with sticks to keep them from straying from the trackway.

The purpose of these long treks across the country was to take animals from farms and markets in Wales to be sold for a higher price at the much wealthier markets in England. A typical drive could take three to five weeks covering several hundred miles. Some drovers headed for the markets in the English Midlands and Herefordshire, while others continued as far as London and even on to Kent.

An important partner in the drive was the Welsh corgi, a working dog kept specifically for herding cattle. They worked the herd from behind in a half circle by nipping at the cows' heels, rather than covering all sides like a sheepdog. They were nimble and, being very low with short legs, they could avoid kicks from the cattle. When the drovers reached the Welsh border on their homeward trip they would set the corgis free to go ahead. These intelligent dogs would then return home, sometimes 100 or more miles.

By its very nature the drive could be an attraction for a local fugitive to flee the area by 'hiring on' as help. The drovers themselves weren't against generating some extra business, and sometimes they would incorporate into the drive 'the odd stray' animal they encountered along the way. However, the drovers were considered to be a generally responsible group, who contributed much to the economy and wealth of the Welsh nation.

The 'porthmon', or head drover, was in charge both of the herd and the sale. He would be responsible for

buying livestock from markets and farms as they passed, and he also had to be bilingual in order to trade with the English. He would often act as a courier, carrying money and documents for local farmers and townspeople to be delivered to addresses in England. Above all else the drovers had to ensure the animals arrived at the English markets in good condition to achieve the best sale prices. This entailed frequent stops for grazing and to rest and water the livestock. Thus the drive progressed at a steady pace covering 10 to 15 miles a day depending on the terrain. Despite this relatively slow pace individual travellers journeying to the English cities often travelled with the drovers for safety. Indeed, by the late 1700s the life of the drover had been so coloured by popular stories as to seem rather romantic. So much so that often the sons of wealthy landowners would join the drives in search of adventure (although one suspects the hard work and tough nature of the drive would soon have taken its toll on them).

Another way that the drovers ensured that the animals arrived at the markets in top condition was to fit them with shoes. Blacksmiths travelled with the drive and their job was to fit iron shoes to the cattle, usually only on the front feet. Sheep and pigs were also treated in this way although in their case they were fitted with a wooden sock with a leather sole. The feet of geese and turkeys were sometimes protected by driving them through a mixture of sand and softened tar. This formed a hard-wearing boot when it set.

Sunday was a day of rest. The animals would need good meadows and pasture and the drover good accommodation and entertainment. As a result, there are drovers' inns dotting the drover routes, some of which are still in evidence today.

It is estimated that upwards of 30,000 cattle each year were driven across the Drovers Roads of the Cambrian Mountains into England to feed the growing city populations during the Industrial Revolution. The drover with his cry of '*Heiptro Ho!*' has been consigned to history by the inexorable 'march of progress', but they contributed much to the economy and cultural heritage of Wales.

10

WELSH MUSIC: FROM THE GREEN GREEN GRASS TO THE GOLDIE LOOKIN' CHAIN

THE LAND OF SONG

It isn't until you live in Wales that you realise one stereotype aimed at the Welsh is actually true. Wales is indeed the 'Land of Song'. The amount of people involved in singing, music and general tuneful noise-making is quite staggering.

Typing 'Welsh Choir' into an internet search engine will produce over 6 million results, and give you information about choirs from Newport to New York, from Pwllelli to Patagonia!

Similarly, there are many places to see live music of all varieties throughout the nation.

'WE'LL KEEP A WELCOME IN THE HILLSIDES' – SOME MUSICAL TRIVIA FROM THE WELSH

So, who has been making a tuneful Welsh noise then?

Dame Shirley Bassey (b.1937), singer
Famous since the 1950s, Dame Shirley has risen to the heights of musical superstardom from an almost destitute beginning in the legendary Tiger Bay in Cardiff.

She recorded three *James Bond* film themes: *Goldfinger*, *Diamonds are Forever* and *Moonraker*, more than anyone else.

In 2003, Dame Shirley held a charity auction at Christies, entitled '50 Years of Glittering Gowns', raising £250,000 for the Dame Shirley Bassey Scholarship at the Royal Welsh College of Music and Drama and a local Children's Hospital.

The Manic Street Preachers, rock band
Welsh rock band the Manic Street Preachers have offered social and political comment through their music since their formation in Blackwood in 1986. With eight top ten albums they have been one of Wales' most successful musical exports.

Lead singer and guitarist Bradfield is virtually unflappable. At what he called 'our greatest ever concert' in the Millennium Stadium in Cardiff on 31 December 1999, a guitar string broke during the last song, 'Design for Life'. Whilst waiting for a replacement guitar, Bradfield continued, telling the audience to 'watch my moves'. The new millennium arrived between 'Motorcycle Emptiness' and 'Can't Take my Eyes off You', performed acoustically by Bradfield (I was there and can confirm it was a fantastic experience).

John Cale (b.1942), musician, composer and record producer
Cale was born in Garnant, Carmarthenshire. He trained as a concert violinist and moved to New York to study classical music.

He founded *The Velvet Underground* with Lou Reed and Sterling Morrison.

Andy Warhol, the leading figure in the Pop Art movement, managed the band. Their 1967 debut album *The Velvet Underground and Nico* has been described by *Rolling Stone* magazine as the thirteenth greatest album of all time.

Cale left The Velvet Underground to embark on what became a greatly influential, avant-garde solo career.

Charlotte Church (b.1986) singer,
songwriter and television presenter
Her 'big break' came when she sang *Pie Jesu* on a TV show in 1997.

Singing arias, folk songs and songs from musicals, as a child she sold more than 10 million records worldwide.

At twelve years old she was the youngest person to have a number one album in the classical charts, with her first album *Voice of an Angel*.

Born in Llandaff, Cardiff, she attended the Cathedral School.

Katherine Jenkins (b.1980) singer
From Neath, Katherine Jenkins is a famous mezzo-soprano who studied at the Royal Academy of Music in London. Her wide range of music, from pop songs to opera and hymns, brought her fame and success as the bestselling classical music star of 2004.

She had worked previously as a singing teacher, a model and a tour guide on the London Eye.

With eight bestselling studio albums and various collaborations, she remains a popular and successful Welsh artist.

Tom Jones (b.1940) singer
The Voice was voted third in a list of *100 Welsh Heroes* (see the entry earlier in this book).

Following his hit single 'It's Not Unusual' in 1965, he has been a household name in the UK and abroad. The single was written originally for Sandie Shaw, another famous popstar of the 1960s.

Jones' friendship with Elvis Presley is well recorded. They met at the Paramount Stage, where Elvis was filming, and there are stories of them enjoying free time together. This friendship endured until Elvis' death in 1977.

In 1974, Elvis introduced Tom Jones at one of his shows with these words of praise: 'There's somebody in the audience I'd like you to meet. To me, he's my favourite singer. He's one of the greatest performers I've ever seen, and the greatest voice, Tom Jones.'

Ivor Novello (1893-1951), actor, composer, singer
During the early years of the twentieth century Novello was famous for his songwriting and musical comedies. During the First World War he wrote the music for the hit song 'Keep the Home Fires Burning' to keep up morale for the troops. He also served in the Royal Naval Air Service himself, narrowly escaping death during *two* crash landings.

He appeared in over twenty-five films and produced a prolific body of work with stars like Noel Coward, Somerset Maugham, Paul Robeson and Siegfried Sassoon.

In Cardiff Bay, there is a sculpture commemorating his life and work. It portrays him sitting working on a manuscript.

Goldie Lookin' Chain
I'm not sure how Ivor Novello would feel about being in a chapter with Goldie Lookin' Chain, but here goes...

The Wikipedia entry for Goldie Lookin' Chain describes them as a 'comedic rap music group based in Newport, South Wales. The group produces controversial and often explicit songs that satirise hip hop, today's consumer society, the 'chav' culture and life in Newport and South Wales in general.'

Their first single 'Half Man, Half Machine' (2004) records the event of one of the band members believing he had turned into a robot, following an experiment with his 1980s ZX Spectrum computer.

With their sideways dig at the American Hip Hop scene, 'Guns Don't Kill People, Rappers Do', they reached number 3 in the UK chart and national success.

No strangers to controversy, a story was released in 2002 claiming they had recorded a single with Charlotte Church – this turned out to be untrue. In 2005 they once again courted controversy when providing entertainment for the World Cup qualifying match between Wales and England: they dedicated their new single 'Your Missus is a Nutter' to Victoria Beckham, who was present with her husband footballer David Beckham. In response, the Welsh Football Association apologised to the Beckhams, although the GLC insisted their tribute had been 'misunderstood', and that it was 'an act of friendship and respect', as a spokesman for the group reported.

The members of the group include: 2Hats, Billy Webb, Mystical, Adam Hussain, Rhys, Eggsy, Mike Balls and Maggot.

LET'S HAVE A CYMANFA CANU

Whether it's from the chapels or churches, the *eisteddfodau*, *gŵyl werin* (folk festivals) or *noson lawen* (traditional Welsh parties), music is all around.

The *Cymanfa Canu* (singing festival) was basically a special service in a chapel. However, the hymns were sung by the congregation in four-part harmony, usually under the direction of a choral director. These would, and still do, take place in ordinary chapels in towns and villages throughout Wales. It is a unique feature of Welsh culture and its preservation is being supported by a number of cultural associations not just in Wales, but throughout the world where the Welsh have settled.

THE WONDERFUL SOUND OF THE MALE VOICE CHOIR

Brighton, London, Oxford, Treorchy! Male voice choirs are one of Wales' best exports. These sometimes fifty-strong choirs are a mainstay of Welsh musical efforts. Even though the last few years have seen something of a decline in new members joining, the recent success of Only Men Aloud has reversed the decline somewhat. Tim Rhys-Evans, a classically trained opera singer and former musical director of the Welsh National Youth Opera, formed the famous male voice choir that rocketed to success after winning the BBC competition *Last Choir Standing* in 2008. The choir is based in Cardiff, and most recently performed 'Caliban's Dream' at the opening ceremony of the 2012 Olympic Games as the Olympic Cauldron was lit.

One of the most famous male voice choirs in Wales is the Treorchy Male Choir. The first recorded existence of a choir in Treorchy was in 1883, when a choir of twenty men won the first prize of £1 at an eisteddfod for their performance of 'Myfanwy' in the Red Cow Hotel, Treorchy. Since then, there have been thousands upon thousands of performances throughout the world: Switzerland, Canada, Australia, USA, Scotland, New Zealand and Germany. There have been records, cassettes and CDs, television appearances and radio broadcasts.

Here's what others have said about the Treorchy Male Choir:

'To hear the Treorchy Male Choir in full throat is one of the great joys of choral music.'

Lord Melvyn Bragg of Wigton, broadcaster

'I sang with the Treorchy Male Choir in their rehearsal room while doing a documentary about Wales for the BBC. It was a wonderful, unforgettable moment and to experience Wales's premier choir at close proximity was a tremendous delight. Your rendering of "The Lord's Prayer" completely devastated me and I had great difficulty holding back the tears. Treorchy Male Choir are *nuli secundi* – second to none. They are in a class of their own and the best choir in the world.'

Brian Blessed, actor

'The Treorchy Male Choir is, without doubt, one of the best known Welsh cultural institutions in the world. I am delighted to congratulate them on providing the voice of a nation.'

Rowan Cantuar / Rowan Williams, then the Archbishop of Canterbury

MUSIC IN WALES

A whole book could be written about Welsh music alone! The history of rock, pop, indie, classical, opera, choirs and brass bands, dance and electronica, folk and traditional, jazz, rap and hip hop is populated with the Welsh.

As they say in Wales...

Can di bennill mwyn I'th nain, fe gan dy nain I tithau.
Sing your grandmother a sweet song and she will sing to you.

PLEASE STAND FOR
THE NATIONAL ANTHEM

There are few national anthems as stirring and memorable as the Welsh one. The Welsh have James James (1833-1902) to thank for the music, and his father Evan James (1809-1878) for the words.

The tune *Glan Rhondda* means *Banks of the Rhondda* and follows a popular music style of the day. James James was a harpist and musician who, according to legend, just imagined the tune as he was walking along the banks of the River Rhondda one day. Arriving home, he asked his father to write some words for him. This he did within a day, and the new national anthem was born, although it was some time before it was recognised as such.

Winning a prize at the national eisteddfod in 1858, its popularity grew, turning into a favourite at large events and gatherings before being eventually developed into the national anthem.

Although usually only the first verse and chorus are sung, here is the whole thing, with the English translation. It gives a sense of the *hwyl* or spirit in the words.

Mae Hen Wlad fy Nhadau

Mae hen wlad fy nhadau yn annwyl I mi,
Gwlad beirdd a chantorion, enwogion o fri;
Ei gwrol ryfelwyr, gwladgarwyr tra mâd,
Tros ryddid gollasant eu gwaed.

Chorus

Gwlad, Gwlad, pleidiol wyf i'm gwlad,
Tra môr yn fur i'r bur hoff bau,

O bydded i'r heniaith barhau.
Hen Gymru fynyddig, paradwys y bardd;
Pob dyffryn, pob clogwyn, i'm golwg sydd hardd
Trwy deimlad gwladgarol, mor swynol yw si
Ei nentydd, afonydd, I fi.

Chorus

Os treisiodd y gelyn fy ngwlad dan ei droed,
Mae hen iaith y Cymry mor fyw ag erioed,
Ni luddiwyd yr awen gan erchyll law brad,
Na thelyn berseiniol fy ngwlad.

The Land of My Fathers

This land of my fathers is dear to me. Land of poets and singers, and people of stature, her brave warriors, fine patriots, shed their blood for freedom.

Chorus

Land! Land! I am true to my land! As long as the sea serves as a wall for this pure, dear land, may the language endure for ever.
Old land of the mountains, paradise of the poets, every valley, every cliff a beauty guards; through love of my country, enchanting voices will be her streams and rivers to me.

Chorus

Though the enemy has trampled my country underfoot, the old language of the Welsh knows no retreat. The spirit is not hindered by the treacherous hand, nor silenced the sweet harp of my land.

Chorus

11

THE WELSH:
WHO ARE THEY?
ALL THINGS WELSH

The Welsh national identity emerged from the Celtic Britons, after the Romans left Britain in the fifth century. Wales is considered to be one of the modern Celtic nations.

The Welsh collectively name themselves '*Cymry*', meaning '*the people of the Land of Cymru*'. These names date back to the post-Roman era, and the relationship of the Welsh with the Brythonic-speaking peoples of northern England and southern Scotland. The Brythonic word *combrogi* means 'fellow countrymen'. Describing the Welsh as *Cymry* was used throughout the Middle Ages and can be traced back to the sixth century, but was probably used before that. The name *Wales* is derived from the word for *stranger*.

The Leek
According to legend, King Cadwaladr of Gwynedd told his soldiers to wear a leek in their helmets when they battled with the Saxons to help them distinguish friend from foe. It reputedly helped them secure the victory. It is also believed that the battle took place in a field of leeks on St David's Day!

The Welsh Guards wear a leek as a cap badge, and tradition has it that they eat a raw leek on St David's Day. The

£1 coin minted in 1985 and 1990 bears the leek in a coronet, representing Wales.

The Daffodil

The daffodil is a popular symbol associated with Wales, but there was some confusion about the Welsh word. The leek in Welsh is *cenhinen*, while the daffodil is *cenhinen pedr* or Peter's leek. Over the years, it seems that they became confused, and both were eventually adopted.

The Three Feathers

The Three Feathers is the heraldic badge of the Prince of Wales. Three feathers emerge from a gold coronet, with the German for 'I serve', *Ich dien,* as well. The badge is sometimes used in rugby to symbolise Wales, but has been rejected by many Welsh as a symbol of the British monarchy, and not Wales.

The Harp

The harp is thought of as the national instrument of Wales. This beautiful instrument first originated in Italy, and first appeared in London in the early seventeenth century. It was quickly picked up by the Welsh living there, and became known as the Welsh Harp.

The Red Dragon – y Ddraig Goch

The flag of Wales bears a dragon, traditionally believed to be the Red Dragon of Cadwaladr, King of Gwynedd, along with the Tudor colours of green and white. It was included in the Tudor royal arms to signify their Welsh descent.

Officially recognised as the Welsh national flag in 1959, it has a longer history than that to Wales and the Welsh. There have been several different theories about *y Ddraig Gogh* – it could have been linked to the Roman period, and military cohorts at the time of Emperor Trajan. It could have been from the mention in the *Mabinogion* the great Welsh saga, where the red dragon fights with an invading white dragon. After a long and winding story, the white dragon is defeated and expelled from the land, leaving the red dragon to rule.

WELSH WORDS THAT ARE COMMONLY USED IN ENGLISH

I bet you didn't know that these words have their origins in the Welsh or old Brythonic languages.

Balderdash: probably from *baldorddu*, a sweet mixture made from flour, milk and eggs.

Bard: from the Welsh *bardd*, meaning 'poet'.

Car or Cart: these are both Welsh words, originally from the Old Celtic *Karrom and Karros*, also giving us the words *carry, carrier and carriage*.

Coracle: from the Welsh *corwgl*, a lightweight boat used in Wales and many other places from India to Iraq, Scotland and Tibet.

Corgi: from *cor 'dwarf'* and *'ci'* meaning 'dog'.

Crag: from *craig* meaning 'rock'.

Crockery: might derive from the Welsh *crochan* meaning a 'cauldron'.

Crumpet: from *crempog* or Breton *Krampoez* meaning 'little hearth cakes' or more correctly 'pancakes'.

Druid: from *derwydd* possibly derived from *'derw'* meaning 'oak'. Or perhaps from the Welsh for 'wizard', *dewin*.

Flannel: is believed to be from the Welsh *'gwalanen'*, a type of wool.

Gull: from either the Welsh or Cornish *gwylan or guilan* which means 'seagull'.

Iron: this word appears to have been influenced by the Old Welsh word *hearn*.

Lawn: derives from the Welsh *Llan* meaning a heath, or area of grass around a religious settlement. It is also linked to the Cornish word *Lan*. *Llandewi* in Wales, or *Launceston* in Cornwall.

Mither: probably from the late seventeenth century, no one is really sure, but it might be from the Welsh *moedrodd* meaning 'worry' or 'bother'. It may also possibly be from the word *meiddio* to 'dare' or 'venture'. In Welsh pronunciation the *dd* sounds like *th* in English.

Penguin: This is possibly from *pen gwyn* in Welsh, meaning 'white head'. Initially, someone mentioned that penguins have black heads, and not white, and this is true. A friend pointed out that this is probably because the name relates to the Great Auk *(Lat. Pinguinus impennis)* but when I checked they had black heads too, with a white bit. So, I've still no idea.

Piebald or Skewbald: from *ceffyl bal*, a horse with a white streak on its face.

BUT WHAT ABOUT THE COCKEREL ON THE CORNFLAKES BOX?

There is a story of Nansi Richards, the famous Welsh harpist, who spent a lot of time in the USA. Upon visiting Will Keith Kellogg, the American industrialist and food manufacturer, in the early 1920s, she mentioned that his family name was very close to the Welsh word *'ceiliog'* meaning 'cockerel'. Kellogg was obviously quite impressed with this. He decided to put a picture of a cockerel on the front of the packaging for his company's product, cornflakes. The link with the cockerel being awake early in the morning worked well with the image he wanted for a breakfast snack. To this day, the green and red cockerel, in the colours of the Welsh flag, could well be another clue to the origins of the cockerel on the cornflakes box.

12

MUST SEE PLACES IN WALES

I'm not going to lie to you, Wales is a fantastically diverse nation, with hundreds of great things to see and do. I think it's best that you just jump in your car, get on a bus, bike or train and find out for yourself ... but these might get you started:

SNOWDONIA NATIONAL PARK, NORTH WALES

The Snowdonia National Park is in the north-west of Wales, and covers a massive 823 square miles (2,131 sq. km).

There are fifteen peaks over 3,000ft (914m), known collectively as the 'Welsh 3,000s', although one peak, Carnedd Gwellianor or Garnedd Uchaf, is not always included because it has the least relative height, appearing as a mere bump on the ridge rather than a separate summit in its own right.

Snowdon (Yr Wyddfa), part of the Snowdonia National Park and one of the fifteen peaks, is the highest mountain in England and Wales, standing at 3,560ft (1,085m). The English name comes from the Old English for 'snow hill', and the Welsh name Yr Wyddfa means 'the tumulus'. It can be climbed in around 3 hours, via one of the six paths. When at the top, you can enjoy some refreshments in the café at the newly refurbished visitor centre.

The opening of the new visitor centre at the summit in 2009 marked the end of a three-year building project. Hafod Eryri was described by the First Minister, Rhodri Morgan, as 'one of the wonders of Wales'.

If you don't fancy walking all the way to the summit, there is a train to the top. The train leaves Llanberis station before it begins the steep climb. There are beautiful views of viaducts, waterfalls and forests as you climb towards the peak. Passing Rocky Valley and Clogwyn station, weather permitting, you can continue to the summit where, on a clear day, you can see as far as the Isle of Man and the Wicklow Mountains in Ireland.

In the rest of the Snowdonia National Park, you can visit any one of a hundred lakes, eighty-nine peaks and 37 miles (60km) of coastline.

LLANDUDNO AND THE GREAT ORME

Llandudno is the largest seaside resort in Wales and has kept much of its Victorian splendour. Since 1864, it has been known as the 'Queen of Welsh Resorts'. The Victorian Pier is nearly 2,300ft (700m) long and was built in 1878. It is said to 'zoom out to the sea ... in spectacular Indian Gothic style rather like a Maharajah's palace floating on a lake'. Every year Llandudno has a three-day Victorian Extravaganza over the May Day bank holiday weekend – with parades and funfairs it's definitely worth a visit. As you might expect, tea shops, fish and chips and good hotels are plentiful in Llandudno.

The Great Orme (*Y Gogarth*) is the great limestone headland immortalised in poetry and prose. It is a nature reserve and home to around 200 feral Kashmir goats, natural wells and possibly one of the most important copper mines of the Bronze Age. There are shops and cafés, a hotel and a play area at the summit. The Great Orme Tramway (one of only three existing cable street tramways in the world) or the Aerial Cable Car (the longest cabin lift in the Britain) can take you to the summit of the Great Orme.

RHOSSILI BAY, THE GOWER PENINSULA AND THE 'RED LADY'

There are 109 Welsh beaches listed in the *Blue Flag Guide*, so it's difficult to know where to recommend. Rhossili Bay does stand out, however, and has been described as 'one of the best 25 beaches in the world' (*The Sunday Times*) and also 'the supermodel of British beaches' (*The Independent*).

Rhossili is a sandy beach stretching 3 miles (5km) in a curve, backed with sand dunes. At the southern end of the bay is the small tidal island called Worm's Head, and at the north is Bury Holms, both of which are only accessible at low tide, when you can also see the remains of several shipwrecks. Rhossili Bay has been used to film *Dr Who* and *Torchwood*, and also featured in the Opening Ceremony of the 2012 Olympic Games, when a youth choir sang 'Bread of Heaven' live from the bay. The sunsets are beautiful.

The Gower Peninsular itself covers around 70 square miles (180 sq. km) from Swansea Bay to the Loughor estuary. As an area of Outstanding Natural Beauty there are many bays, beaches and villages.

There is more to this area than natural beauty, however, it is also a place of significant historic interest. Wales has been inhabited since the Upper Paleolithic era (50,000-10,000 years ago) and there have been archaeological finds of global significance. In 1823 archaeologists found a skeleton in the coastal Paviland Cave. They named their find the Red Lady of Paviland, and, at the time, it was the oldest human fossil to be found anywhere in the world. It remains the oldest ceremonial burial in Europe to be unearthed.

More recently, scientists discovered that the *lady* was actually a man, and the bones were dyed red with ochre. Ornaments, shells, ivory and mammoth bones buried along with the body confirmed that this was an important burial. Although now on the coast, when the burial took place the sea would have been more than 60 miles (100km) away and Britain was still attached to the European mainland. This would mean that the burial place would have been one of the highest points for miles, and the views would have been spectacular.

CARDIFF BAY

Undergoing a huge transformation over the last few decades, the bay is considered to be one of Britain's most successful regeneration projects. In the 1980s it was suggested that the mostly derelict docklands could be redeveloped to provide Cardiff with much needed homes, a shopping area, restaurants and cafés and, last but not least, a centre for the arts.

To enable this to happen, a barrage would need to be built across Cardiff Bay from the docks to the seaside town of Penarth, creating a freshwater lake, fed by both the Ely and Taff rivers. Cardiff Bay has one of the greatest tidal ranges in Britain; the water level drops over 45ft (14m) at low tide. This means that the docks would have been inaccessible for almost fourteen hours each day. The new barrage would make the waterfront accessible at all times.

It was hoped that if the new area were a success, it would become a symbol of the economic redevelopment of Wales' capital city. So construction began on the £220 million barrage, including lock gates, sluice gates, and even a fish pass. It was 1999 when the 0.68-mile (1.1km) barrage was completed, and with it about 500 acres of the muddy flats of the old docks became a bay.

Since then £2 billion has been spent transforming the area – to become what we see today.

The Wales Millennium Centre (Canolfan Mileniwm Cwmru) opened on 29 November 2004. Hosting opera, comedy, dance, ballet and musicals, this building bears the words of Gwynneth Lewis, the inaugural National Poet of Wales, boldly declaring *Creu Gwir Fel Gwydr O Ffwrnais Awen* (In These Stones Horizons Sing).

Close to the Millennium Centre is the Senedd, the home of the National Assembly of Wales' debating chamber. The democratically elected body represents the people of Wales and makes laws for Wales. Opened in 2006, this environmentally sound building harvests rainwater, has natural ventilation, a light,, a biomass boiler and an earth heat exchanger system. The assembly is open to the public – you can watch debates or take a tour of this extraordinary building.

The third building, within a few moments' walk of the Senedd, is the Pierhead Building. This historic building housed the administrative office of the Port of Cardiff, and incorporated the Big Ben of Wales, an imposing clock tower facing the sea. The fully refurbished and renovated building is now home to an excellent Welsh history museum, displaying several important artefacts, including the binnacle from Scott's ship the *Terra Nova*, which sailed from Cardiff on the British Antarctic Expedition in June 1910. The museum is also home to the Pennal Letter sent by the Prince of Wales, Owain Glyndwr, to King Charles VI of France in 1406.

Did you know? The new BBC Wales drama studios in Roath Lock are the home of *Doctor Who*, *Casualty* and Welsh language drama *Pobol y Cwm*. Roath Lock is also the place where Captain Scott embarked on his ill-fated expedition to the South Pole in 1910.

There is also the *Doctor Who* exhibition, boat trips around the bay and beyond, the Norwegian church Roald Dahl's family attended, and an unofficial fan-shrine to another Welsh-filmed BBC drama, *Torchwood*.

If none of that appeals to you, in total Cardiff has 149 pubs, bars and nightclubs (eighteen of them on the waterfront), seventy-three restaurants and 125 hotels.

TENBY

This beautiful walled seaside town in Pembrokeshire is named Dinbych-y-Pysgod in Welsh, meaning the *little fortress of the fish*. The town has a long history, probably dating back to around the ninth century. The town flourished as a holiday destination, just as the Wye Valley did, during the time of the Napoleonic Wars, when travel on the Continent was dangerous and ill-advised.

With sandy beaches to the north, west and south, the walled town of Tenby continues to attract a significant number of holidaymakers each year, staying in the bed and breakfast accommodation and hotels throughout the town, and a little further afield in caravan parks and camp sites. The nearby Caldy Island is home to a small village, a monastery and a Cistercian community, originally from Scourmont Abbey. They moved to Wales in 1929. The monks produce perfume, shortbread and chocolate to supplement their income. Their lavender perfume was said to be 'simply the best on earth' in a guide by Luca Turin published in the *London Evening Standard* in 2008. The community receives visitors to the beautiful and tranquil island throughout the summer months.

Without a doubt this picture-postcard town and the island are an excellent destination for a weekend break or a longer holiday.

BRECON BEACONS

Without a doubt, the Brecon Beacons National Park is a beautiful part of Wales, visited by some 3.8 million people a year. There are castles, towns, wonderful landscapes and great scenery. The park is named after the Brecon Beacons *(Bannau Brycheiniog)*, a row of peaks including South Wales' highest point Pen y Fan standing at 2,900ft (880m).

The national park was created in 1957, and stretches from Pontypool in the south-east to Llandeilo in the west, and Hay-on-Wye in the north, covering 519 square miles (1,344 sq. km).

Don't forget to visit the Ystradfellte Waterfalls. The waterfalls and caves, and the blue pool (Pwll Glas) and limestone gorges offer a great place to stop off on any tour of the national park. Or maybe a walk in the Black Mountains? The mountains stretch across the border into Herefordshire at the eastern side of the national park, and start in Abergavenny with The Sugarloaf and The Skirrid, the 'Holy Mountain'. Raymond Williams, in his historical novel *The People of the Black Mountains,* wrote of the great history of the mountains, as home to the Vikings, Romans, Saxons and Normans:

> See this layered sandstone in the short mountain grass. Place your right hand on it, palm downward. See where the summer sun rises and where it stands at noon. Direct your index finger midway between them. Spread your fingers, not widely. You now hold this place in your hand.

THE MYSTERIOUS ISLAND OF ANGLESEY (YNYS MÔN)

Anglesey is a county off the coast of north-west Wales which includes the Isle of Anglesey itself and Holy Island where the town of Holyhead is found. With an area of just over 270 square miles (714 sq. km) it is the largest island in Wales and the sixth largest island surrounding Britain and the largest in the Irish Sea.

ANGLESEY, ANGLESEY, SO GOOD THEY NAMED IT ... SEVERAL TIMES

The name Anglesey dates back to the tenth century and derives from the Old Norse meaning Ongull's Island, although it was many years later when the name was adopted by the Anglo-Norman invaders during the invasion of Gwynedd. The suggestion that the name is derived from a link with the Angles has been discredited.

And if that wasn't enough, the Welsh name Ynys Môn has quite a history too. It is derived from the early British *Enisis Mona*, and during the first Roman era it was called *Mona*. Rather romantically, it was also called *Môn Mam Cymru* or 'Mother of Wales' by Giraldus Cambrensis, because it was declared to be so fertile that it could produce enough food for the whole of Wales.

Finally, there are several old Welsh names for the isle:
Ynys y Cedairn – The Isle of Brave People
Ynys Dywyll – The Dark Isle
Y fêl Ynys – The Honey Isle

It is unsurprising that the island has so many names, because it has featured in so much of the history of the region.

STONES, DRUIDS AND ROMANS

Some of the oldest stones in the world are found on Anglesey, dating from the Pre-Cambrian period, and there is evidence of of human settlements from almost every chapter in history.

Many megalithic monuments and menhirs are scattered around Anglesey, and there are twenty-eight cromlechs (megalithic monuments) that remain on the uplands overlooking the sea.

Anglesey is most famous for being the home of the druids. They were an influential force for all the people and commanded a significant amount of respect. In AD 60 the Roman general Gaius Suetonius Paulinus resolved to crush them with military power. In a surprise attack, he deployed the amphibious Batavian contingent and marched steadily across the island, destroying sacred shrines and groves. The druids were unable to hold off the Romans, and it looked like they would be consigned to history.

However, news of Boudicca's revolt reached the general and the contingent were forced to fall back. The druids were able to rebuild and regroup, holding off invasion for another eighteen years until AD 78, when Gnaeus Julius Agricola was declared Roman Governor of Britain and Anglesey became part of the Roman Empire.

There is still some evidence of the Roman invasion of Anglesey in some disused copper mines, the foundations of Caer Gybi, a fort at Holyhead and the present road from Holyhead to Llanfairpwllgeyngyll, which might have been a Roman road.

After the Romans left Anglesey in the early fifth century, pirates from Ireland moved in, so Cunedda ap Edern, a warlord from Scotland, drove the Irish out; this took until AD 470. The town of Aberffraw became the capital of the Kingdom of Gwynedd, and apart from a damaging Danish raid in AD 853 it remained the capital until the thirteenth century.

SO ... WHAT ABOUT MODERN ANGLESEY?

It's a beautiful place. The entire coastline was declared an Area of Outstanding Natural Beauty in 1966 and features

MENAI SUSPENSION BRIDGE

many beautiful sandy beaches, especially between the towns of Beaumaris and Amlwch and along the western coast.

There are two bridges connecting Anglesey and Holy Island to the mainland, the Brittania Bridge and the Menai Suspension Bridge, which was designed by Thomas Telford in 1826.

Anglesey is relatively low-lying compared to the mountainous region of Snowdonia, not many miles away. The towns of Llangefni, Menai Bridge, Holyhead, Llanerch-y-medd, Amlwch and Beaumaris are unique and have interesting histories. Beaumaris (Biwmares) in the east of the island, for example, features Beaumaris Castle, built by Edward I as part of his 'Bastide Town' campaign in North Wales. The town of Amlwch, in the north-east of the island, was once largely industrialised, having grown during the eighteenth century supporting the copper-mining industry at Parys Mountain. The town of Menai Bridge (Porthaethwy) in the south-east grew substantially when the first bridge to the mainland was built, in order to accommodate the construction workers. Until then, the town had been one of the ferry crossing points to mainland Wales. A short distance from the town lies Bryn Celyn Ddu, a Stone Age burial ground, and the village with the longest official place name in the United Kingdom, *Llanfairpwllgwyngyllgogerychwyrndrobllllantysiliogogogoch*.

Tourism is now the most significant economic activity on the island. Agriculture, especially dairy farming, provides the secondary source of income for the island's economy. It should also be noted that Anglesey is home to an olive grove, the most northerly one in the world.

Anglesey has the second highest percentage of Welsh speakers at 70 per cent.

Don't forget to visit the castles too!

FACTS ABOUT WELSH CASTLES

There are over 400 castles in Wales.

The most famous castles were built in the reign of the Plantagenet King Edward I (1272-1307).

Flint, Rhuddlan, Builth, Aberystwyth, Caernarfon, Conwy, Harlech and Beaumaris castles were all built during this period.

Welsh castles are easily identified by their stronger keep or main tower, a high wall, several outer walls or baileys, several gatehouses and moats sometimes in complex concentric shapes.

Incidentally, Beaumaris Castle is considered the best example of a concentric castle in Europe. It has been a World Heritage Site since 1986.

Welsh medieval castles were fantastically expensive to build. Caernarfon Castle cost Edward I £27,000 to build – that's the equivalent of around £50 million today. Part of a chain of fortifications, this castle was constructed on the site where the Celtic tribes used to live and the Romans even had a settlement there. On the traditional route from Ireland, via the Menai Strait and Anglesey, this is the site for many historic and legendary episodes in Welsh history. It is linked with the saga of the *Mabinogion* and the heroic actions of Welsh heroes.

Flint Castle, which is now in ruins, is the only British castle with two dungeons. It is famous for having the thickest walls of any castle in the world, being 23ft (7m) thick.

Caerphilly Castle is the largest castle in Wales, built between 1268-1271 by Gilbert de Clare to stop Llywelyn ap Gruffudd's campaign in the south. It dominates the centre of the town and has been variously been partially demolished and restored over the centuries. The castle covered over 30 acres (120,000 sq. m) at one time, making it one of the largest in Europe.

The historic St Donat's Castle was sold in 1925 to the newspaper publisher William Randolph Hurst, who built America's largest newspaper network. He bought the castle as a gift for his mistress, Marion Davies, spending a fortune renovating the property, even buying whole rooms from other European castles to bring to St Donat's. This lavish castle had many famous guests during this period. Arthur Conan Doyle, Charlie Chaplin, Bob Hope, John F. Kennedy and George Bernard Shaw all visited and stayed in the castle.

Carreg Cennen Castle is surely one of the most spectacular in Wales. Set on a limestone crag, towering above a lush green valley, it has been called one of the most romantic places in Wales. It is one of the few privately owned castles in Wales. Due to a legal error, the castle was sold to a Gwilym Morris, as part of farmlands. Upon finding their error, the Cawdor Estate tried to buy it back for £100, but the family decided not to take up the offer. The ingeniously adapted castle is protected by pits, drawbridges and gatehouses, with a natural cave incorporated into the defences. Despite this, however, Carreg Cennen fell to Owain Glyndwr's forces.

Flint Castle was the first castle built by Edward I. It dominates the harbour estuary on the River Dee. Three thousand men were employed in building the structure. This masterpiece of military architecture continued to grow for ten years before work stopped. It was meant to be even bigger, but never reached its intended size.

When castles were abandoned, they became scrapyards for the local community. Have you ever wondered why houses built around derelict castles always seem to be constructed in the same stone?

SOME CURIOUS FACTS ABOUT WALES AND THE WELSH

Did you know? Newport, the newest city in Wales, was granted a royal charter in 2002. It is home to one of only two working transporter bridges in Britain, and one of eight in the world. A suspended gondola crosses the River Usk with towers on each bank of over 240ft (74m) in height. It is recognised as a symbol for the city.

Did you know? The prefix to place names *Llan* in Wales, doesn't mean a 'church', but rather a 'consecrated area', a holy area, set aside for a particular religious purpose.

Did you know? In Llangadwaladr there is the oldest royal tombstone in Britain. It marks the burial place of Cadfan ap Iago, King of Gwynedd from AD 616 to AD 625.

Did you know? The Great Glasshouse at the National Botanical Garden of Wales in Llanarthne, Carmarthenshire, is the world's largest single-span glasshouse. Designed by Norman Foster and Partners, it looks like a giant raindrop.

Did you know? Wales looks a lot like China! The 1958 film *The Inn of the Sixth Happiness* with Ingrid Bergman was shot in Gwynedd, but was set in China. Also, *Lara Croft Tomb Raider: The Cradle of Life*, starring Angelina Jolie, was shot in Snowdonia, but was also set in China.

Did you know? Many films have been shot in Wales. The war scenes for the Hollywood blockbuster *Captain America: The First Avenger* were shot in Caerwent, near Chepstow. Also, *Harry Potter and the Deathly Hallows parts 1 & 2* were also shot partly in Wales. Dobby's shell cottage appeared in Freshwater East, Pembrokeshire, in 2009. Most recently, the film *Snow White and the Huntsman* was filmed on the beautiful Marloes sands, also in Pembrokeshire, early in 2012. Previously the location was used in 1968 for the film *The Lion in the Winter* which starred Peter O'Toole, Katharine Hepburn and Anthony Hopkins.

Did you know? Julia Gillard, the Prime Minister of Australia, was born in 1961 in Barry, South Wales. She suffered from bronchopneumonia as a child and her parents were advised that it would aid her recovery if she lived in a warmer climate. This led the family to migrate in 1966.

A FEW MORE
WELSH IDIOMS AND PROVERBS

A fo ysgawn gallon, ef a gân	The light-hearted will sing
Po callaf y dyn, *anamlaf ei eiriau*	The more sensible the man the least often the words
Rhoi halen ar ei gynffon	Put salt on his tail *(tell someone off)*
Cof a llithr, llythyrau a geidw	Memory goes, letters stay
Dawnsio ar y dibyn	Dancing on a cliff *(playing with fire)*
Caiff dyn dysg o'i *grud i'w fedd*	Man learns from cradle to grave
Cenedl heb iaith *yw cenedl heb galon*	A nation without a language is a nation without a heart
Cymro glan gloyw	A shining clean Welshman *(a committed Welshman)*
Gorau adnabod, *d'adnabod dy hun*	The best knowledge is of yourself
Gwell dysg na golud	Education is better than wealth
Dipyn o dderyn	A bit of a bird *(a ladies man)*

Fel ci efo dau gynffon

Like a dog with two tails
(very happy)

Gwell swllt da na sofren ddrwg

Better a good shilling than a dud sovereign

13

WELSH SAINTS

What has Merthyr Tydfil got in common with San Francisco and Buenos Aires?

Well, that's a good question, and the answer isn't obvious. It is that they are all named after saints. San Francisco is named after St Francis of Assisi, the twelfth-century Italian friar and teacher. Buenos Aires has the full name Ciudad de Nuestra Señora Santa María del Buen Ayr, meaning our lady of the fair winds, after a statue of St Mary was rescued from the sea. Merthyr Tydfil, according to legend, is named after St Tydfil, a daughter of King Brychan of Brycheiniog, who was murdered by pagans around AD 480; the place was subsequently named Merthyr Tydfil in her honour.

The period of Welsh history between the departure of the Romans in the fourth century and the invasion of the Normans in the early eleventh century is one shrouded in mystery and speculation.

The fifth and sixth centuries in Wales are referred to as the Age of Saints, and much has been written on the spread of Christianity under the care of these Celtic saints. These unstoppable missionaries travelled the roads and seaways between Wales, Ireland, Cornwall, Brittany and the Basque country to spread the Christian faith.

The inscribed tombstones and crosses bear witness to this extraordinary age where the Welsh were indeed a religious people, led by some amazing characters.

The place names that begin *Llan*, like *Llandudno*, *Llandewi*, *Llanelli*, *Llanbradach* and the 600 others, refer to what could have been a religious site, possibly the beginnings of a church, or a burial ground. It previously would have referred to tribal enclosures. To this day, the famous monastic sites of St David's, St Illtud's and Llantwit Major continue to provide artefacts of early Christianity that are some of the most important in Britain.

M. Gray, in the *New Welsh Review* No. 52, perfectly describes this age, and its effect on the Welsh people:

> The lives and traditions of the Welsh saints are inscribed on maps and on our sense of national identity. When the Sacred Land Trust embarked on an attempt to list some of the sacred landscapes of Wales, they were eventually obliged to admit that, for the Welsh, the whole land, can be sacred. Settlements named after local saints, holy wells, pilgrimage routes and standing stones testify to a pervading sense of the sacramental in the very fabric of our country.

SAINT DAVID – DEWI SANT – PATRON SAINT OF WALES

Of course, we should start by thinking about St David, *Dewi Sant*, that superhero in the world of Welsh saints. We know quite a lot about his life, in contrast to some of his fellow saints in Wales.

If you are lucky to be in Wales on St David's Day (1 March) you will find the whole nation in a festive mood. School children dress in national costume; churches and chapels hold services and social events. Welsh food is cooked and people wear daffodils to remember the life of the saint, and all that is good about living in Wales and being Welsh.

A bishop in the sixth century, he wasn't regarded as a saint, or the patron saint of Wales, until sometime later. David was a native of Wales and was probably born in the mid- to late fifth century; it seems that he lived a reasonably long life, and died on 1 March AD 589.

St David is said to be of royal lineage. His father, Sant, was the son of Ceredig, who was Prince of Ceredigion, a region in south-west Wales. His mother, Non, was the daughter of a local chieftain. Legend has it that Non was also a niece of St Arthur.

St David was born near Capel Non (Non's chapel) on the south-west coast, near the city of St David's. We know that he was educated in a monastery called Hen Fynyw; his teacher was Paulinus, a blind monk. St David stayed there for some time before taking a party of followers on missionary journeys.

St David established several churches; he also travelled to Cornwall and Brittany. It is also possible that he lived in Ireland for a time. Two colleagues of his, Saints Padarn and Teilo, are said to have accompanied him on his journeys.

St David was sometimes known as *Dewi Ddyfryr* (David the water drinker) as drinking just water was an important part of his life. He also used to stand up to his neck in ice-cold water as an act of penance. The monastery at Glyn Rhosyn or Rose Vale, where the cathedral of St David's stands today, was the home of a brotherhood that David founded. The regime was strict, with hard physical work farming accompanying the long monastic day. The monks also had to feed and clothe the poor and needy.

Many of the stories of St David are found in the work of his hagiographer (autobiographer to the saints) Rhygyfarch, who tells us that David's best-known miracle occurred when he was preaching to a crowd in the village of Llanddewi Brefi. A synod had been called there to choose an archbishop. A great crowd had attended, and people found it difficult to hear or see David. One of the crowd shouted, 'We can't see or hear you!' At that moment, the ground rose up under his feet to create a small hill. A white dove then appeared on his shoulder, the traditional Christian symbol for the Holy Spirit. Quite unsurprisingly, David was then elected archbishop.

As an aside, and if you're thinking that you've heard the name of the Welsh village Llanddewi Brefi previously, it's because it was made famous again by the BBC television series *Little Britain*, where the character Daffyd Thomas (*sic*) a 'ridiculously obtuse character', who believes himself to be the 'only gay in the village', accuses his fellow villagers of homophobia. Anyway, enough of that – back to the life of St David…

It is claimed that St David lived for over 100 years. According to Rhygyfarch, his last words to his followers, in his sermon the previous Sunday, were 'be joyful and keep your faith and creed. Do the little things.'

The phrase 'do the little things' (*Gwnewch y pethau bychain*) is a very well-known phrase in Welsh today, and serves as an inspiration to many. David was buried in the grounds of the monastery, where the cathedral now stands.

Giraldus Cambrensis, Gerald of Wales, who travelled through Wales in the twelfth century, also wrote about St David's early life, noting how widely known he was throughout the whole Christian world.

ST ELVIS

You might not know, but the Welsh have a St Elvis, who was the cousin of St David, and baptised him at a church near Haverfordwest in Pembrokeshire. The parish is apparently now the smallest in Britain, consisting only of the church, St Elvis' Farm, St Elvis' Holy Well and St Elvis' Cromlech (prehistoric tomb), and off the coast are the St Elvis Rocks. Dr Peter Williams, writing from the USA in 2000, noted that:

> St Elvis is only one of hundreds of Welsh saints of the 5th and 6th century, a time when the light of Christianity shone

brightly in Wales after having been extinguished over all of Europe, a time when England was still pagan. It was a time when Christianity itself was in danger of disappearing, the survival of the church in Wales creating a bastion from which Ireland was first converted, and from the Irish missionaries, the rest of Europe.

He goes on to mention that over 100 Welsh saints are associated with their leader Arthur, long before the legends had taken hold in France. Truly Wales was a land of magic, mystery and romanticism producing stories that have stood the test of time. Dr Williams continues:

It was a time when the stories of Arthur and Guinevere, of the Holy Grail, Tristan and Isolde, Merlin, the Fisher King, the Black Knight, the Green Knight, and of all the famous knights associated with Camelot and Avalon came into being, and all originating in Wales. Wales certainly seems to have not only the oldest surviving language in Europe, but also the oldest Christian heritage; for in the first millennium it was accepted by Rome as the 'cradle of the Christian Church'.

Many have written extensively on the Welsh saints, all-important historic places, Roman temples, Celtic crosses, burial grounds and the earliest settlements and chapels; they chart the history of the saints in Wales and the history of the people of Wales.

Here are some more Welsh saints, and their extraordinary stories:

Paul Aurelian

St Paul Aurelian was a sixth-century Welsh saint who became the first bishop of the See of Leon, and one of the seven founder saints of Brittany. The links between Wales and Brittany are quite astounding. The ancient seaways were like medieval motorways, exchanging culture, tradition and trade between the nations. Paul Aurelian is said to have died at the ripe old age of 140, and was said to be a 'preserver of the faith, constant lover of his country, champion of righteousness' ... and a vegetarian. He was also one of the seven founder saints of Brittany.

Beuno

St Beuno was the grandson of a Welsh prince who brought his niece back to life. Her name was St Gwenffrewi (St Winifred). Eleven churches and his well-known monastery are evidence of his missionary zeal and hard work.

Did you know? St Beuno's is a Spirituality Centre found in North Wales, not far from Rhyl. Built in 1848 as a place of study for Jesuits, little has changed structurally. However, today it is a place of retreat for anyone who needs to investigate or deepen their Christian faith. In November 2009, the BBC filmed at the centre, allowing five volunteers to experience a silent guided retreat. The programme *The Big Silence* was a hit, allowing people to think about taking time out of their busy lives to think about life and faith.

Cadoc

One of the heavyweights of the saintly world is St Cadoc. Born at the end of the fifth century, he became the Abbot of Llancarfan near Cowbridge in South Wales. His monastery was famous throughout the whole British Church as a centre for learning. Many Welsh saints received their theological education here at the feet of St Cadoc. His *Life of Cadoc,* written in the Norman era, is particularly important because it contains historic markers to the life of King Arthur. Cadoc was the son of Gwynllyw (Woolos), the enigmatic ruler of South Wales. Gwynlllyw led a band of 300 warriors who enjoyed a bit of pillaging and raiding. Cadoc didn't want to join the family business so he joined the Church. He was a missionary to areas of Wales, Scotland and Brittany, visiting religious communities far away. He even travelled to Rome and Jerusalem. His father later retired to a hermit's life with his wife Gwladys and gave up his violent ways.

Derfel

St Derfel was born around 566 and was one of seven knights of King Arthur who survived the Battle of Camlann. This battle was reputed to be the final battle of King Arthur, who was mortally wounded by his enemy Mordred. The battle probably took place in Somerset, but could have been Cornwall or even Falkirk or Gwynedd, such is the cloud that surrounds all things Arthurian. Derfel, the legendary warrior, was immortalised in the medieval Welsh poetry of Tudur Penllyn, when he wrote:

Derfel mewn rhyfel, gwnai'i wayw'n rhyfedd, Darrisg dur yw'r wisg, dewr yw'r osgedd.

(Derfel in war, he would work his spear wondrously, steel covering is the garment, brave is the appearance.)

Elen

St Elen's story is told in one of the great tales of Welsh folklore: she was the daughter of a chieftain and is said to have introduced the Celtic form of Christianity into Wales from Gaul. She is remembered for persuading the great Roman leader Magnus Maximus (Macsyn Wledig to the Welsh) to build roads across Wales to help them defend themselves from invaders. Therefore she was acknowledged as the patron saint of road builders and travellers long before St Christopher.

Govan

Born in AD 500, one legend has it that St Govan was an Irish monk, who in old age travelled back to Wales to find the friends and family of the abbot who had trained him as a young monk. Apparently pirates attacked him on his journey, forcing him to hide in the rocky gaps of the cliffs in west Wales. He decided to stay there and live within the small cave he discovered.

Did you know? To this day, the cave can be reached by following a long flight of stone steps. There is a thirteenth-century chapel built of local sandstone. That isn't where the mystery of St Govan stops, however; there are legends that tell the story of him being one of King Arthur's knights, Sir Gawain, who is believed to have taken Holy Orders in later life after a violent and dangerous life as a knight.

Illtud

St Illtud was born in the fifth century and his life is full of fantastic legends. Born in western Brittany, according to his biography he was 'a most wise magician, having knowledge of the future'. Taking up arms for King Arthur, he attacked the abbey at Llancarfan, and was chased into a bog by the monks, who seemed to be quite handy with swords too. His whole party sank and drowned in the bog, all except St Illtud. Taken back to the abbey, he was reminded by St Cadoc that he was supposed to be a Christian, and the embarrassed warrior repented and took up the monastic life. Illtud's pupils included St Gildas, Paul Aurelian, Patrick and even David.

Melangell

St Melangell was the daughter of an Irish king. Her father expected her to marry a nobleman. However, she refused, vowing celibacy, and fled to Wales. Legend has it that she didn't see the face of a man for fifteen years until one day she met Brochwel Yscythrog, Prince of Powys, who was hare hunting on his land. Chasing a hare into the thicket, he found Melangell, with the hare hiding in her robes. The prince was amazed at her beauty. After listening to her story, he gave her substantial lands and money to build an abbey. She built it as a sanctuary to all those fleeing from trouble.

Petroc

St Petroc was reputed to have made pilgrimages to Rome and India, taming wolves and converting thousands to Christianity. He was born in Wales around AD 560, the son of a Welsh king. He studied in Ireland then moved to Cornwall. There are several dedications to him throughout Devon and Cornwall, where he set up several monasteries. The flag of Cornwall is dedicated to St Petroc.

Tysilio

St Tysilio was a Welsh bishop, scholar and prince. He was a great authority in Wales during the turbulent seventh century. His father forbade him from becoming a monk so he fled to Meifod Abbey. Eventually the abbot persuaded his father to let him take Holy Orders. He started his training and became a great evangelist, travelling throughout Wales. He returned to the abbey to take over as abbot. After his brother's death, he was ordered to marry his widow and take the throne of Powys. He refused and eventually fled once again, this time across the channel to St Suliac, founding another monastery there, where he died in AD 640.

Did you know? Today he is remembered in several places in Wales, but none more important than the village with the longest place name in Britain. The interestingly titled 'Llanfairpwllgwyngyllgogerychwyrndrobwllllantysiliogogogoch', which translates into English as 'Saint Mary's Church in the hollow of the white hazel near a rapid whirlpool and the Church of St Tysilio of the red cave'. There are hundreds more saints, each with stones to tell of this great land of Wales. Indeed, there is so much more to tell you, but sadly we've run out of space. This is, after all, a 'Little Book of Wales'.

YOU ARE NOW LEAVING WALES –
PLEASE TAKE YOUR LITTER WITH YOU

So there we have it, our journey through Wales is complete! That doesn't need to be the end of your journey though; go to visit Wales and see for yourself how great it is. From the north to the south, the east to the west, it is truly an extraordinary place.

YMA O HYD

If you enjoyed this book, you may also be interested in…

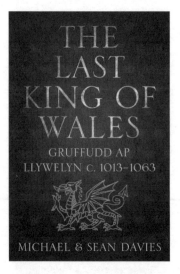

The Last King of Wales: Gruffudd ap Llywelyn
c. 1013-1063

MICHAEL & SEAN DAVIES

Born in northern Wales in the early part of the eleventh century, Gruffudd ap Llywelyn seized an unprecedented amount of influence in a ruthless ascent to power. After forcibly unifying all of Wales and claiming the title of 'king', Gruffudd successfully attacked the English with the help of a Viking contingent. This is the first popular account of the only king to rule all of Wales as a single country and also the last king of the ancient Britons.

978 0 7524 6460 2

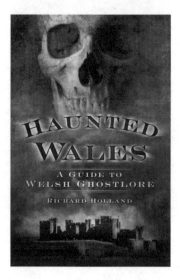

Haunted Wales: A Guide to Welsh Ghostlore

RICHARD HOLLAND

Wales is a fearfully haunted place. It abounds in castles and mansions, ancient churches, lonely lanes and crossroads, even bare mountainsides which can lay claim to a resident spook or two. The ghosts of Wales are bold and memorable, striking in appearance, forceful in character, often terrifying and sometimes even dangerous. Prepare for a fascinating county-by-county tour of hundreds of ghostly encounters from one of the most haunted countries in the world.

978 0 7524 6058 1